A Tale of Two Cancers

(and a bit of a Stroke)

1. Foreword

Readers, if you are new to my journey...

In my first two books, *Fifty Shades of Gray Matter* and *Learning to Love Your Stroke*, I took a light-hearted view of my stroke, interspersed with some serious personal insights for Stroke survivors and their families. This, my third book, finds me back at home after three months in hospital being treated for cancers, but this time without my much-missed, late wife Elaine to assist me. I openly acknowledge Elaine was extremely instrumental in my stroke recovery as I adapted to living with a debilitating condition. This time, however, I need to rehabilitate on my own. Nevertheless, I remain positive about the outcome and my future mobility even as the now, proud owner of Spinal tumours and Prostate Cancer – Hence the book title.

The title of this and my other books might suggest I don't take life, or myself, too seriously, which is true, but I also hope my stories give the reader an insight into the survivability of disorders previously considered as life-ending; give a taste of how I faced my demons and overcame adversity in my determination to stop being pigeonholed as an invalid, and how humour and humility has helped me face life-threatening cancers.

As the title to my book may suggest, I was diagnosed with cancer in 2020, and after a couple of sessions of radiotherapy and some hard-core cancer medication to manage the prostate cancer, followed by intense physiotherapy, I was discharged home to rebuild my life. I stay confident in my outlook on life and, once home, joked that I have been discharged more times than Royal Navy Destroyer guns during a period of austerity, following both the Macmillan Cancer Nurses and the Stockport Social Services deciding they could no longer help me after a review of my progress had clearly demonstrated I was on the way to self-sufficiency. This is not to say I do not experience daily struggles, but when these occur, I just visualise what Elaine would say to me during a struggle, and generally it would be something *encouraging* like, "Stop whinging, and get on with it." So, I do. She loved and managed me for 44 years, and continues to do so!

My first book *50 Shades of Gray Matter* tells the story of my response to a severe stroke, and how - with the help of Elaine and my children - I was able to reach a level of recovery that allowed me to volunteer at my local stroke ward mentoring new stroke survivors, some of whom I am still in contact with to offer advice and support. Additionally, it tells of how I had started to rebuild my life, re-joined the gym, and started to make a weekly visit to my local pub for a couple of post-stroke beers.

My second book, *Learning to Love Your Stroke*, picks up my recovery following the loss of Elaine after a marriage of 41 years. The narrative also details the idiosyncrasy of the impact of erroneous neural messages that affected my recovery and how I overcame them. The book additionally highlights the importance of family to a stroke survivor's recovery - both the good and bad! Also featured is the anecdote of a stroke survivor who was in hospital at the same time as I was as an inpatient, whose family pushed back on the notion of physiotherapy when the survivor was tired. My intention of recounting this story was to reflect that the early stages of a stroke recovery set the foundation for an individual's future capabilities, so it is critical that the family actively encourage participation in the physiotherapy programme rather than take the *perceived easier or kinder* option of declining physio support. I was fortunate that Elaine and my children would take the time to watch my first faltering steps, admittedly whilst enjoying my obvious incompetence, but always with good humour and encouragement, and never let me miss a physio session irrespective of my desire to do so. I will always be grateful for being pushed and encouraged by my family in those early days. I believe I had made good progress with recovery from my stroke, and life was good, other than for the loss of Elaine, until the spinal tumour made an unexpected and unwelcome entry into my life – more of which later…

The final part of book two encourages stroke survivors to return to their pre-stroke activities, if at all possible, to regain a semblance of what used to be, and as a motivation for to them to work even harder to recover their former lives – or find acceptance in their altered state. As an example of this, I recount how my daughter arranged for me to use a putting green not far from her house in Derby on a weekend break in a hotel, as part of my first faltering steps to return to my life as it used to be. A far-cry from weekends spent as a member on one of the best golf courses in Stockport, Romiley Golf Club, albeit as a less than average golfer, but the feeling when I successfully putted a 30 yard putt (the distance gets longer with every telling!) will stay with me forever. I felt wonderful and a touch emotional as the ball dropped into the hole, and encourage every stroke survivor to enjoy a walk (or hobble) down memory lane as part of their recovery.

I felt just as euphoric when I received a message from another stroke survivor who had been in hospital at the same time as I was. John had read my book, *Learning to Love Your Stroke*, specifically the chapter on returning to pre-stroke activities. John wrote to me, "*Your book arrived this morning, so far a riveting read. You've managed to put into words most of my thoughts and actions over the past nearly five years. I am aware all strokes 'are different' but ours seem pretty similar. My main focus is getting to drive again, and with the help of Motability, I will get a stroke assisted car within the next couple of weeks. Hopefully, this will awaken parts of the brain which have become dormant. Thanks again for taking the time to put in words the battle stroke survivors face. You truly are inspirational.*" The thought that my book helped someone feel better about themselves and their stroke, reaffirmed my belief in the worth, value and potential impact of sharing my story.

As well as writing my books, during my time in hospital, I decided that I should produce a daily update of my life and treatment in hospital following diagnosis of my cancers. Writing this daily blog had a selfish element to it. I come from a large family and the thought of communicating to multiple siblings and their offspring when I could post a single (hopefully humorous) blog to keep them informed - and thereby off my back (!) - had massive appeal.

Those of my readers who have enjoyed my first two books will know Elaine and I met whilst we served in the Royal Navy, where for me with a surname of Wilson, I was always known as *Tug Wilson* after an 18th century admiral famed for improving the life of the common sailor. My navy nickname was combined with the messages we received from family when on overseas deployment, affectionately known as *Family-Grams*. So my *'Tug Grams'* were born to offer daily updates on my cancers, provide details of my progress with treatments, and deliver anecdotes about the various locations I found myself in. The early Tug Grams were intended to give my two children and siblings a light-hearted take on my life dealing with cancer, however thanks to the power of social media, Tug Grams spread to reach friends as far afield as Scotland, Yorkshire and Cornwall, as well as those in my international bubble in Portugal. It was the brainchild of my niece and Editor-in-Chief, Becky, to use the Tug Grams as the basis for my third book.

For those who have not read my previous books, Elaine and I met at the Royal Navy Communications School in Hampshire. I was a fully-fledged sailor of three year's Navy service, whereas Elaine was a trainee Wren completing her communication skills training, and who, as part of her training course, attended the typing class I supervised as part of my duties. Ironic really, because Elaine was always a better typist than me, and called me sausage fingers due to my large hands when compared to her dainty hands. Anyway, we met on her first evening at HMS Mercury, the communications school, and remained together for her nine weeks training, seeing each other every night except for the mandatory Wrens Mess cleaning night every Monday when they were confined to barracks to clean their living accommodation as part of their training regime. At the end of her nine weeks, just prior to her departure for her first draft having successfully completed her training, I told her our relationship was over. She was moving away, and I was due to join a new ship which meant our time together was limited; however, as I watched her class of Wrens being driven away from HMS Mercury to board a train to London from the local station in Petersfield, the sight of Elaine sobbing as she waved goodbye hit a chord I had never experienced before. I resolved that as soon as I finished work the following day, I would catch a train to London, go to the Wrens Quarters in South Kensington, and beg forgiveness for my stupid mistake in ending our relationship. Luckily for me, Elaine was as forgiving then as she was throughout our time together - we reconciled and spent the next 44 years together.

Elaine and I married in 1977 following which Elaine resigned from the Wrens in line with Navy regulation at that time, which discouraged married couples remaining in the service. I continued to serve on different ships, predominantly based overseas in the West Indies (a tough gig, but someone had to do it). During this period we lived in Navy Married Quarters in Chatham, home of HM Ships Eskimo, Ashanti and Tartar, before transferring to a quarter in Kings Langley near Watford while I was based at NATO Headquarters in Northwood. I was anticipating a married overseas appointment when I would have been able to take Elaine with me. Instead, despite every box ticked to say it was my least preferred option, I was drafted to Submarines. That was the final straw for me. I was spending too long away from Elaine as it was, so the thought of long periods away incommunicado forced my hand, and I too resigned. Following my decision to leave the Navy, we made plans to buy a house in Elaine's hometown of Stockport. I did give her the option to move back with me to my council estate in Liverpool, but that didn't seem to appeal and therefore Stockport it was.

Many years later, much water under the bridge, numerous lockdowns, and many words written, this book will be published in the midst of my cancer treatments. My spinal tumour surgery appears to have been successful. My primary prostate cancer, whilst incurable, is treatable and carries with it a long life expectancy if the treatments are successful. To date, my longevity signs are favourable. More importantly, this book will be my first account of a recovery without Elaine providing the practical encouragement that was so pivotal in my progress with my stroke.

My situation has been compounded, like it has for so many in the UK, by the isolation created by the Covid-19 pandemic and associated lockdowns. Covid cut swathes through my recovery planning and execution, but I remain optimistic that whilst things are difficult for us all, they will return to normal before too long, and we will be able to get on with our lives once more. The most difficult aspect of the lockdown or isolations for me, as I am sure for many others, is the lack of physical contact with family. I like to think my Naval training left me with a mindset of "hunker down, and stay calm" until things that you have no control over stabilise, and life returns to normal. Nevertheless it is tough, and brings home to me on a daily basis that I am missing my *wing-woman*, Elaine.

Sadly, too many of us will have heard, or will hear the life-changing announcement that they or their loved ones have been diagnosed with cancer, even more unfortunate some will be informed of a far more serious form of cancer than mine. I hope my story goes a little way to convince cancer sufferers that they can still laugh at their condition, and can embark on a recovery journey with one finger most definitely pointed upright!

2. From Little Acorns: Medical Diagnosis

My journey with cancer started just as my stroke green shoots were taking hold. My walking was improving over longer distances, and I was able to walk with a more natural gait and without the drop-foot associated with stroke survivors. I was able to make regular trips to the gym, when Covid allowed, for much needed physical respite. I had also decided after I returned from Surrey, where Elaine had passed away, that I would get back behind the wheel of my car, and return to driving to give me greater scope and freedom for a return to a more normal life. During my time as a Sales Manager, I frequently drove 20,000+ miles a year around the UK so getting back behind the wheel was a logical step in my recovery, but also a significant milestone for me.

Driving sorted, recovery making good progress, life was positive. I was arranging to visit friends in Portugal as soon as Covid permitted, and as a family we were planning another Christmas in Surrey at my son, Rob's, house. Rob, daughter-in-law, Ellen, and my two granddaughters, Olivia and Sara, would be there, as well as my daughter, Jenni, and her partner, Chris. It promised to be a traditional Christmas. At this point in time, we made plans for the festive season encouraged by the words of the then Health Minister: Covid was in retreat.

At that time in September 2020, I thought the only blot on the landscape would be that for my second Christmas, I would be without Elaine, and our children, Rob and Jenni, would be without their mum. Just goes to show you, you never know what is around the corner.

The first indication that something was amiss with me, I dismissed as being a symptom of getting old, or to be more truthful that my bed was getting old. I would get out of bed in the morning feeling every one of my 64 years, and it seemed to take forever to unwind my back to regain a semblance of a normal posture. The pain was a constant niggle, but one I was able to control with paracetamol and heat-pads. Equally, I reflected that I hadn't changed my bed or mattress for many years so took steps to purchase a replacement bed.

The back pain got progressively worse over 3-4 weeks leading me to conclude I had overdone things in the gym, so I rested for a week with no exercise. This seemed to give some respite so the following week I returned to the gym, only for the backache to return with increased ferocity. Taking painkillers seemed to have little effect on what was a constant pain, never enough to stop me doing things, but a constant reminder that all was not well.

I had already successfully used a masseuse who came to my house to address post-stroke issues with spasticity - a neural condition I experienced down my left side as a result of my stroke. Weekly deep tissue massages left me for the first time in four years able to enjoy a night's sleep without the interruption of limbs doing a painful rendition of RiverDance, so it was a logical next step to ask Aneta to work her magic on my back problem. Surprisingly with the benefit of hindsight, the massage offered some initial respite, though this soon wore off.

Things came to a head following a visit to the gym. I had driven to the gym, walked from the car to the entrance, some 40-50 metres, and undertaken a one and a half hour gym workout which involved a 0.5Km unaided walk on the treadmill as well as weight and TRX exercise for those familiar with gym equipment. Suffice to say, a good workout. Once finished, I walked back to my car to drive home. I felt good, if not a bit tired, as I made myself a cup of tea following my training, totally oblivious to the events that would unfold over the next 12 hours.

I walked unaided with my drink into the lounge to catch up on the midday news on TV and ponder what to make for my lunch. Decision made, I went to rise from the settee, only for my legs to collapse under me. I assumed I had overdone things at the gym so decided to rest for 30 minutes before I ventured to my kitchen for my luncheon choice of fruit and cheese. Half-hour later, I stood only for my legs to once more refuse to cooperate, leaving me to reach the uncomfortable and frightening conclusion that I was possibly experiencing another stroke. The counterbalance to this alarming thought was that whilst my legs were disobedient, my face appeared to be unaffected, and whatever was attacking me was affecting both legs rather than the one side normally associated with a stroke, so once more I decided to do nothing and rest for a further 30 minute period.

This time when I stood my legs had transgressed from disobedience to outright mutiny, so with all thoughts of lunch forgotten, I made my way to the bathroom by furniture surfing and arm-walking the walls. As I made my way back to the lounge in a similarly unconventional manner, I resolved to call my doctor and seek medical advice on what I still believed (but intended to ignore until I had to address) was another stroke.

Getting through to the doctor was easier than I thought, maybe because of my medical history, but I was soon speaking to a young doctor and trying to give an objective assessment of my symptoms. Dr Higgins was very calm and reassuring as she listened to my symptoms, and didn't, as I had thought she would, advise me to take some painkillers and rest for a while. Instead she arranged an immediate video call with me, probably took one look at my *'rabbit in the headlight'* stare, and told me she was going to seek a second opinion from another doctor. Within minutes, Dr Higgins was back on the phone telling me in her calm manner that because of my medical history, she recommended I dial 999 and seek an emergency ambulance. This I did, but we were at height of the pandemic with ambulances stacking outside Accident & Emergency units, or out of action to allow deep cleaning once a patient had been accepted into A&E. For whatever reason, I waited 7 hours for an emergency response with an increasing and unrelenting pain in my back. The waiting time did, however, give my daughter time to travel to the family home in Stockport from her home in Derby so at least she was able to make hourly calls to the ambulance service for them to conduct a telephone stroke assessment, and by their own admission drop me down the response list when unsurprisingly I passed the telephone stroke risk assessment.

Whilst I fully appreciated the strain the NHS was operating under during this period of the pandemic, it was nevertheless an incredibly stressful wait for the paramedics to arrive, not least because I still believed I had suffered another stroke and knew time was of the essence to begin treatment on a stroke. Additionally, the pain was ramping up to the extent that painkillers offered no respite. The paramedics, when they arrived, were courteous and professional but questioned why I had been waiting for so long when they reviewed my blood pressure, which on their arrival was 200/175 against the normal reading of 140/80. They quickly completed a few more checks, all of which were a blur for me, before wheeling me to their waiting ambulance and blue-lighted me to the North-West Stroke unit at Salford Royal Hospital. Luckily for me, their immediate priority was to reduce my blood pressure so I was strapped in and connected to an oxygen tank breathing in the same gas and air mixture normally reserved for women giving birth for the duration of the 30 minute drive.

Despite the short drive, it was incredibly painful to lay flat on a stretcher, so I was grateful when we rushed into the hospital A&E department. Whether the result of the gas and air during my transit, or my natural optimism, I had convinced myself that I was suffering with nothing more serious than a disc problem, which would be quickly resolved with a painful, but effective cortisone injection to the affected area, and I would be home for breakfast.

Despite my optimism, I retained a niggle of doubt that something sinister was going on; the total loss of leg functionality caused me growing concern, but I tried to suppress the doubts and joke my way through A&E. My act wasn't totally convincing though which led to the first of many acts of kindness that I was to experience from the wonderful staff in the NHS. This time, the simple act from an Australian nurse who held my hand as we made the journey from A&E to the stroke ward. She reassured me that I would be okay, and that a Stroke Consultant would come to see me as soon as they were free.

True to her word, just after 9am, a female consultant with an entourage of young male doctors entered my side ward and began a physical and cognitive examination, which included a rectal examination of my prostate. As I lay on my side, my female consultant had the good grace to laugh out loud when I announced, "I don't normally do this on a first date" as she probed and investigated. She then tested my limbs and cognitive reactions before announcing, "I'm almost 99% positive that this is not a stroke, but to be absolutely sure I want to schedule a brain scan and a full body scan" she ordered of her entourage before leaving me to rest. I was subsequently transferred to a side ward to rest, safe in the knowledge that my dodgy disc would be identified and corrected following the scans. I would be lying if I didn't admit that a second stroke was still circling the periphery of my consciousness. After all, the consultant was only 99% sure, and I still had to consider the loss of my limb function. Roll on those scans.

3. The Early Days: Salford Royal Foundation Trust

Even though I had been transferred from the A&E department to the stroke ward, I still harboured the hope that my condition was something other than a second stroke. Playing on a loop in my mind was the statement from a patient's wife on the Stroke ward in Stepping Hill Hospital nearly six years previously, that the "second stroke was almost always the killer" - that announcement came shortly before her husband passed away following his second stroke. Not surprising then that I was hoping for a different outcome than stroke, but still I believed stroke was the likely cause of my current predicament.

Brain and spinal scans completed, I was transferred back to the stroke ward and advised that my consultant would review the scan results and let me know the outcome. In the meantime, I was confined to my bed, and was only allowed to sit upright to eat or wash by raising the bed so my spine was always flat against the mattress. The Tug Grams had yet to see the light of day, but in one of my early social media messages, I commented that the ward staff had discovered I was not a *patient patient* as I ignored advice and attempted to recover from my condition, which prompted the following message on 2nd October:

I think the nursing staff are realising I'm not a patient patient, but trying to smile and be polite. Just had my first ever bed bath, really don't know why people fantasise about it.

Morphine was being administered to me every four hours so the pain was under control, which left me able to focus on my recovery, albeit through a drug-filled haze. I was still of the opinion I had experienced a second stroke, and was mindful of the need to put weight through my recalcitrant limbs to ensure I reprogrammed neural pathways destroyed by the stroke that I still believed was the cause of my limb degradation. At this time, after three days on the stroke ward, I had not been given any feedback on the scan results, and though I was reviewed by doctors on a daily basis, they appeared more interested in what I could do with my limbs rather than tell me what was wrong. The fact the daily Salford Royal tests were reminiscent of the tests I underwent on the Stroke ward some years previously simply reinforced my belief that I had experienced another stroke, so my focus was to rebuild neural pathways and put weight through my limbs.

To say my focus put me at total odds with the ward staff was an understatement. I would take any opportunity to stand upright and put weight through my legs, which would immediately result in the ward management berating me and telling me I had to remain in bed and stay still.

I would like to think I remained polite, but I refused to accept these instructions. I knew from my previous stroke that it was imperative I use my limbs whilst I had a level of movement. I kept thinking of one of my early physiotherapists using the mantra "use it or lose it", so was determined to follow this advice, and really could not understand why the medical staff on B3 Stroke ward couldn't see the benefit my actions would have on my eventual recovery. It was only later that evening that Lauren, the Staff Nurse, asked me what I knew of my condition. I explained that I hadn't been told anything, but assumed it was another stroke, hence my insistence on movement and mobility whilst on the ward. Lauren asked me to promise to remain still in bed if she committed to getting a doctor to come and see me. Seemed like a fair deal, so I resigned myself to remaining flat in my bed, whilst Lauren carried out her part of the bargain.

True to her word, Lauren made some calls, and a young doctor came to my bedside, pulled the curtains round, and asked what I had been told. Again I reiterated that I hadn't been told anything and remained in the dark regarding a formal diagnosis, but that I suspected a second stroke hence my focus on recovery. He apologised that I had not been briefed before now, and announced that I had definitely not had a stroke. My brain scan was clear which left me euphoric; the fact I hadn't experienced another stroke filled me with a deep sense of joy – this, coupled with the copious amounts of morphine, ensured my concentration was less than complete as he went on to explain that they had found something amiss on my spine.

My social media post on 3rd October reported:

Just had initial results from my spine scan, they have found something amiss so want to do another scan that will give greater clarity - so it's back in the torpedo tube this afternoon. Looks less likely to be a stroke as Spine Consultant feels I have good and equal movement/strength in my limbs. Seems bizarre to be happy when told I have a potential spinal issue, but I am so pleased it is unlikely to be a stroke, and hopefully when I get the brain scan results later, I will have a definitive answer.

The narrative that I had something amiss with my spine continued for another couple of days, but I remained overjoyed that it wasn't another stroke so I was happy. It was only comments from doctors that they were consulting with colleagues at the Christie, an oncology specialist hospital, which started to raise a red flag in my mind. What followed next was 'Diagnosis by Innuendo' - nobody seemed to want to voice my condition aloud, so I received various messages indicating something sinister was going on with my spine. Messages that inferred dialogue with experts at the Christie without ever really expressing what I was suffering from. It was only when I had a visit from the Spinal Consultant, who asked for permission to complete a biopsy on the tumour on my spine that cancer became a reality. Whether I was in denial, or more likely under the influence of morphine, all I could think of in answer to his question seeking permission for a biopsy was, "I wonder if anyone has ever said 'No, you can't" before I nodded my consent. Even then in my shocked state, I was thinking the biopsy would be a small procedure and a few days away, so was totally unprepared when he responded to my consent with a definitive, "I have booked a theatre for Sunday (a few days hence); hopefully, we will know more after that".

My daily blog on 4th October recounted:

Just been briefed by the doctor, in essence; Salford Royal trying to find me a bed in a specialist Spinal unit, either here or Stepping Hill, and the plan is to move me ASAP. The urgency is my spinal cord is being compressed and that is why my balance and gait is being affected. The referral to a spinal unit is because that is also where they house the oncology specialists and it is possible the compression is being caused by a cancerous growth. Upshot is the spinal cord neural messages are being zapped or misrouted hence the loss of

balance etc. Got that news and then Liverpool went 1-0 down, don't know what is more upsetting.

Until they complete a CT scan they won't know for sure, but they believe it likely to be a secondary cancer causing the compression. I must admit I feel better knowing there is a reason for my Bambi on Ice impressions. All feels a touch surreal but I am determined to keep my feet firmly on the ground (even if I can't feel the floor) and not start to react until I have the full facts xx

Everything had just become real, and I asked the ward staff if I could be wheeled to an office to call my children and tell them the news. I also asked the Consultant if he could speak to my next of kin as I wasn't sure that I would remember the medical details of my condition, given every discussion with the medical teams contained an inordinate number of medical terms, and I was still morphine intolerant.

I made the call to Rob and Jenni to advise them I had been diagnosed with a tumour, whether from shock or morphine, I don't know, but the details of my condition given to me by the medical staff had been totally erased from my mind. Luckily, I had anticipated this by asking the Consultant to speak directly to my next of kin, unfortunately he delegated to a member of his team who called my children and re-entered 'diagnosis by innuendo' and told Rob and Jenni that I had possibly an infection or maybe something else on my spine. Needless to say, Rob and Jenni held onto the hope that whatever I had was just an infection. When I spoke to the Consultant later that day and asked for clarity, he advised unequivocally "You have a tumour and we need to operate urgently because it is pressing against your spinal cord, and we are worried it could cause permanent damage".

I reflected to myself that I was happier with the innuendo! But took solace that the biopsy was imminent, so then we would know for sure.

My blog on 6th October stated:

So the verdict is a tumour on my spine, they are going to do more tests over the next few days (which I thought was positive, as it means I've got at least another week to live). The consultant did mention lots of "Loma's, which went right over my head, but he is going to ring Jenni and have a full & frank discussion with her which will be helpful all round.

My biopsy had been brought forward to Friday, and I would be 'nil by mouth' from midnight the previous evening and then scheduled to go to theatre early afternoon for what I thought would be a quick keyhole 'slice and dice' before I was given the results of the biopsy. I was quite positive; some would say blasé when I wrote on the 9^{th of} October:

Morning, well I'm washed, shaved and dressed in a rather fetching hospital gown ready for the theatre. When they said let's get you dressed for the theatre, I had a vision of Top Hat & Tails, but this'll have to do - My Limo picks me up at 8.30, will message again later x

The nurse during preparations to go to theatre was Erin, a young student nurse, but one whose early twenty-something years belied a compassion and empathy far beyond her age. I am pleased to say I have kept in contact with Erin and am looking forward to the successful completion of her training and for Erin to become a fully badged nurse. As Erin prepared me for surgery – I still thought of it as a quick keyhole procedure – she offered words of encouragement and asked me if I wanted her to tell my family when I departed for, and returned from, theatre. I gratefully accepted her offer, and asked her to telephone Jenni. Throughout that morning waiting to be taken to theatre, Erin would pop over to see me between her duties to see that I was okay and if I needed anything. Erin was the first of many nurses I met during my three months in hospital who delivered a level of care and compassion that was amazing and beyond the call of duty, made even more so by their workload in the midst of a pandemic. I did then, and still now, remain in awe of the maturity and empathy shown by Erin, and later Lauren, another trainee nurse I encountered at the Devonshire. Both young ladies are a credit to their profession and made me believe that for all the talk of its future demise, the NHS cannot fail with people like Erin and Lauren coming through. As if to reinforce her commitment to the profession, Lauren even had the surname Nightingale!

As I waited to be taken to theatre, I posted:

Hi, turns out they will do everything today, not just a biopsy. I'm 2nd on the list today, going to Theatre early afternoon. Op will take 4-5 hours, and will include fitting of metal pins to strengthen spine. May take a while to fully come round from the Op, so don't expect too much by way of updates today.

Eventually, after what seemed like an absolute age, a porter arrived to wheel me to theatre for what I still believed was going to be keyhole surgery. The anaesthetist, an aptly named, but unrelated, Doctor Wilson and the surgeon arrived to start to draw hieroglyphics on my back, and explain in matter of fact voices the procedure I was to undergo, and what they wanted to achieve. I can only remember the words "cut open", and "install metalwork to support the spine" before I drifted into a deep sleep instigated by the mixture of anaesthetic administered by Doctor Wilson. It truly felt like seconds before a gentle voice was saying, "Hi Philip, how are you feeling? I'm just going to dab your lips with water as you may be dry and we need you to start to rehydrate". I felt fine, although apparently in someone else's body, as I couldn't move, and when I tried the pain was incredible. The same gentle voice broke through my thoughts and explained I was on the recovery ward, the operation had been a success and once I was fully conscious I would be moved back to the ward. The nurse, whose name I didn't notice, asked me if I had any questions, I wanted to ask why my mouth was full of cotton wool, and why my back was so painful after keyhole surgery, but my mouth was so dry my questions came out as a mumbled incoherent noise. The nurse continued to talk in a soothing voice whilst dripping water onto my lips, and into my mouth to rehydrate me as I continued to come round from the anaesthetic.

I have no idea how long I spent in recovery, drifting in and out of sleep, but each time I awoke I felt slightly more normal, albeit mindful that it hurt when I moved, something I still couldn't reconcile with keyhole surgery. Shortly after I had a visit from the surgical team who carried out the procedure, I later shared: **Well still alive so that's a bonus, and Op went well xx**

Around this time, on our 'The Wilsons' WhatsApp group, which has my many siblings, partners and numerous offspring in, messages of concern, comfort and encouragement were being exchanged – at this early point, Rob and Jenni were my intermediaries. One early 'motivational' message came from one of my sisters:

Rita, sister, on The Wilsons WhatsApp: At this rate, I may just add a get well message to Xmas card to Phil.

Moved back to the ward, where the first order of the day was a cup of tea. I must have still been delirious from the anaesthetic because I expected to be greeted by Erin with an update of her call advising Jenni, but I quickly realised that I had been gone so long the day shift had left and I was now in the capable hands of the night shift.

I messaged the morning of 10 October: **Morning. Reasonable night's sleep given I was hacked into yesterday and had a Meccano 'fix' on my back. Seriously though pain massively reduced thanks to copious amounts of morphine, and though too early to see improvements in movement, feeling very optimistic xxx**

Later that day, the nursing staff and physio team attempted to get me upright and try a few steps, I wrote: **Hells bells, just done my first physio since I arrived, not been that unsteady since "Splice the Mainbrace" at the Spithead Review in 1977. Then I drank industrial quantities of pusser's rum, then went ashore, very messy night.**

My movement is seriously degraded, but they are saying they caught the tumour early, so I should make a good recovery. Had I left it much later, I could have lost all lower limbs functionality, which is a frightening thought. That said they think for all of my stroke recovery work, because this was medically invasive, it will take much longer to recover, but hey ho, done it once.

Ironically I opted to stop the morphine mid-afternoon today because I didn't think I needed it anymore. Fast forward 3 hours and I was like a addict outside a methadone clinic - *Glad to say the morphine is now kicking in so yes, still very sore, but then I had a 6 hour procedure so I shouldn't be surprised xxx*

The other shock to my system following readmittance to the hospital ward was the fact I now had a couple of body attachments in the form of two drains in my back, which I immediately nicknamed "Shiraz & Merlot" in addition to a catheter, necessitated by the need for me to remain still in the short term.

At least my new attachments gave me something to do other than count the ceiling tiles, which was to see which of my 'bottles' would fill first.

Rob, son, on The Wilsons WhatsApp: Just spoke with dad, he's up to his tits on morphine so very happy.

4. Diary of a Cancer Patient: Tug Grams

Sunday 11th October 2020 saw the emergence of the *Tug Grams* when I wrote:

Tug Gram 1

Not a good day, lot of pain. Doctor been round. Changed my pain medication to give me 12 hourly doses of the strong stuff. Have low blood pressure so need to up my water intake. Left side quite weak and painful but they think they is because I am starting rehab, but they are pleased I am giving it a go. Not much else they can do, need time for body to accept the havoc they have wreaked removing the tumour, then for the body to start to heal. Best wait until tomorrow when hopefully will have a better day. xxx

Not the most coherent message, and probably reflective of the high dosages of morphine I was being given, nevertheless the start of my long association with my daily family messages. Things seem to have improved when I wrote on Monday 12th October:

Tug Gram 2

Not a great night, no pain thanks to my new best mate Mo Feen (morphine), but because they have discontinued my anticoagulant medicines to allow the wounds to heal, I am at greater risk of clots and more strokes, so I wear massage pads on my legs to constantly agitate the muscles to prevent clots, unfortunately whilst they may keep me alive, they also keep me awake all night!! At least I can sleep during the day - Can tangibly feel the strength returning to my left side, and I'm getting movement back which is great. Not quite ready to join Jen in her 30 mile training runs, but soon maybe... Feel so much better today :) enjoy your day :)

My outlook was definitely improving as I saw small but positive progress in my condition, with that I was able to bring humour into my daily blogs.

Tug Gram 3

YAY!!! 5 hours uninterrupted sleep even whilst wearing my vibrating welly boots!! It might have longer, but I was found by a vampire around 5AM. Even though she was dressed like the ward sister, I knew she was a vampire because she was desperate for my blood and it had to be done before the day shift came on (daylight right!), I've watched too many House of Horror vampire films to be fooled by such obvious subterfuge :)

Once the blood had been sucked from me, it was time for the superhero to make his appearance in the form of the Mo Feen - He might not score goals like Mo Salah, run like Mo Farah, but if Carlsberg did superheroes, Mo Feen would be right up there.

Had one of the drains removed from my back yesterday, did have 2, I classed them as Shiraz and Merlot, and in truth they did look good enough to drink, but I would probably have been in competition with the vampiric ward sister.

Having a post Mo Feen cup of tea, feeling good and looking forward to what the day will challenge me with. Bring it on!

Tug Gram 4

Another great night's sleep, assisted without doubt by copious amounts of my mate Mo Feen, but it ensures I wake to this day considerably more positive than I left yesterday.

My lack of positivity was in the main a result of lots of physio yesterday. Physio that for someone used to overachieving on rehab was less than effective. Mo Feen may have done his job, but his rapper pal's Mo Billy T and Mo Shun were noticeable by their absence. My marching on the spot would have had the Regimental Sergeant Major of the Coldstream Guards shoving his Bearskin where the sun doesn't shine.

Luckily, I spoke to Rob & Jenni and they reset my expectations, and they reminded me it is only 4 days since major surgery, additionally my x-Navy friends Lucanne, Pat & Julie added their words of encouragement, one of them added me I couldn't March as a 15 year old, so what did I expect at 64!

Anyway a new day, already looking forward to the PT doing their worst. All of my drains and cannula have been removed - so the worst pain I can expect today is the ripping off of miles of sticky tape covering the myriad of pinpricks in my hands and arms!

Tug Gram 5

Can't believe it has been 2 weeks since I took up residence here at Salford Royal. Can't say it's passed quickly, but it's certainly been memorable.

Another good night's sleep, woke once just after 1 am, and thought I'll never get back to sleep with the noise on the ward, the next thing it was 6.30 and I'm being woken for a blood pressure reading.

Physio showed a marginal improvement yesterday, but I'll take that. In a world of fine margins even the slightest improvement is to be welcomed. My balance remains as precarious as Boris Johnson's decision making, but I am determined to work on it today and if that means I can stand upright for a few seconds without demolishing a couple of nurses, that'll do! :)

The litmus test will be when they take me for an X-ray on my back - assume they are checking for missing surgical instruments - anyway I have to stand totally unaided for about 30 seconds whilst they take the X-ray. Could be a long session. Got visions of the results appearing on the X-ray equivalent of "It'll be alright on the night" as they take different shots of my collapsing body as I attempt to stand without support - I feel it's going to be a defining day today. Let's do this!

Jenni, daughter, on The Wilsons WhatsApp: Hi everyone, just letting you know dad is doing a load of rehab through the day so he is knackered.

Tug Gram 6

Another excellent night's sleep, even more memorable by the fact Mo Feen was nowhere to be seen. Not a drop of the hard stuff but slept like a baby :)

Will today be the day for my great balancing X-ray? Who knows, could easily get gazumped again by others with greater priorities, but if it does take place it will be another tick in the box of the great escape plan

Shall look forward to Physio today, in the absolute belief that today I will nail it. No more Bambi on Ice, today I shall be Rudolph Nureyev, gliding across the floor like a Chieftain Tank with one track missing - Happy Friday everyone, it's going to be a good day.

Jacqui, sister, on The Wilsons WhatsApp: It's lovely to hear Phil's voice in his words. Sounds like he's in good spirits. Sending love to you all xxx

Nicola, niece, on The Wilsons WhatsApp: I would like to request video footage of the physio today please. I wanna see him glide.

Tug Gram 7

Admittedly it was Mo Feen assisted so won't count as a world record, but slept from 10.30pm until 6.30am this morning. Out flat until a nurse woke me to change position in bed. You know you're getting old when you are forced to change positions because of a risk of bed sores, rather than when you are younger and you simply turn a page in the Kama Sutra!

Seem to remember the Rappers Mo Billy T and Mo Shun doing a cover version of "I can Fly" during my sleeping period. It sticks in my mind because it was at odds with my vibrating wellies duetting with "these boots are made for walking"

So X-rays completed yesterday, it was all of the twisting and turning (No, not another reference to the Kama Sutra) that necessitated the Mo Feen last night. I think today's excitement is a visit by occupational health - the ward equivalent of the Jehovah's Witnesses - they come in groups and hand out hospital versions of the Watchtower like "Hitting the floor safely" or "PHD courses for putting your socks on unaided"

Anyway it's Saturday, there's a dilemma! Do I go out or stay in tonight? Mmmmmm tough one, but on reflection may just stay in!

Tony, brother, on The Wilsons WhatsApp: Very amusing text.

Tug Gram 8

Rita, sister, on The Wilsons WhatsApp: Is anyone else as disappointed as me? Ran downstairs this morning for the latest update from Phil – no text!!!

And on the seventh day God finished his work that he had done, and he rested. So God blessed the seventh day and made it holy, because on it God rested from all his work that he had done in creation.

Men stopping toiling in the field, Money lenders stopped trading in the temple (at least until the Sunday Trading Laws of 1994), and Patients shall rest in their beds. - Actually made up that last bit about the patients resting, we rest 24/7, 7 days a week so Sunday is a normal day for us so maybe we should make Sunday different by having a boogie day, a day when we cast off our cannula and shake a wicked welly. On second thoughts that would probably fill the hospital morgue faster than a person with Covid released back into the community!

So maybe I'll just lie here and think of what I would normally do on a Sunday. Oh yeah SFA - So lie back and think of England while you count the ceiling tiles :)

Tug Gram 9

Monday morning, Day 19 in the Big Brother House. Have a feeling this is going to be a momentous week. Should have my biopsy results back, which will probably say it was just wind - I'm going to smash the rehab, and my standing upright will be as safe and secure as hiring Prince Andrew as your babysitter - it's going to be a great week :)

Tug Gram 10

So when the doctor asked me what I knew about my Prostrate, it appeared that my answer of it scores 11 at scrabble wasn't what he was looking for. So began a 20-minute discussion culminating in the fact I am now the proud owner of Prostate cancer (wonder what it will fetch on eBay?). Have to confess I didn't take a lot in, in fact the only thing that stuck in my mind was my Moobs would get bigger. Not the best-selling feature he could have brought to the table. (Must have a chat with him about his sales technique).

So I can wallow in self-pity or move on, and whilst for a short period self-pity had a certain appeal, moving on got the popular vote. So today we are going to smash physio and do some marching on the spot that would make an old soldier weep at the sight (Can't guarantee that will be because of the quality of the footwork. I'm more likely to be standing on his toes)

So here's to another day on the Costa del Salford

Becky, niece, on The Wilsons WhatsApp: When my Dad was being checked for prostate cancer, I remember learning that it's one of the slowest growing cancers (like, several years) and one of the most treatable.

Tony, brother, on The Wilsons WhatsApp: When I say keep the spirits up, does not mean go on a bender xxxx

Tug Gram 11

Day 21 in the Big Brother House, here on the Costa Del Salford. The new format is like a cross between I'm A Celebrity - without the Bush-trucker trials, and Strictly - when the only dance on show is the Zimmer Frame shuffle, as we look to regain the poise & flamboyance of our youth whilst swirling round the ward held up by two physiotherapists. The only rules on I'm A Celebrity appear to be how many times in a shift patients ask badly overworked, and stressed-out nurses "Do you know who I am"? and "What is wrong with me?"

Oh for the opportunity to be able to respond on behalf of these frazzled nurses. I make allowances for the really poorly who are just desperate for relief of any kind (Been there, got the t-shirt and it's not nice, luckily, I also had my mate Mo Feen). The people I take exception to are those who whine for the sake of whining. For those I award a one-way ticket to Dignitas with no refund :)

So what have I learnt in the past 24 hours? Well I learnt I cheat at Scrabble, my 11 points for Prostate, should have been 10!!! I blame the Freudian fear I have of being asked to lie on my front, hearing those chilling words, "this may feel a little cold" accompanied by the snap of rubber gloves being engaged in a threatening manner - to think some people do this for fun - for entering Prostrate into the scrabble checker instead of my new condition.

Talking of which it would be a much fairer system if we could select our illnesses based on their scrabble scores. We'd quickly eradicate the likes of measles with a low score of 9, instead we would focus on cures for the likes of Typhoid which scores 16. :)

The other thing I've learnt is that the strength in my legs is returning. I stood for the best part of an hour at the wall bar yesterday, exercising and contemplating the day ahead. Feeling very pleased with myself until I remembered that it was standing at bars for extended periods that caused my stroke in the first place.

Looking forward to Physio today, although at the risk of whinging myself, I have to confess conversation with my Zimmer frame as I glide gracefully round the ward, is like those mumbled words during the last slow dance at the Navy base bop. You're more interested in what might follow rather than meaningful wordplay as you step on her toes for that agonizing 3 minute smooch. :)

Tug Gram 12

It seems my escape plans are getting closer to fruition, just need to decide whether to go over the wall on my bike - Not sure my BMX has the lift, alternately I could dig a tunnel but the thought of walking around the hospital (especially given I still don't have the full power in my legs) with all of that extracted soil down my shorts in an effort to surreptitiously redistribute the soil round the ward doesn't cut it - the cleaner whinges if you move something on your bedside table. So God knows what her reaction will be to a load of loose soil everywhere.

Maybe I should revert to plan C - Let the doctors tell me I'm well enough to go home.

Phase 1 will be the nuclear scan on Friday. I've been scouring the news to see that Sizewell A is not missing, and I've read all about the Salisbury Novichok murders so I can identify if the FSB try to inject anything other than friendly radioactive material into my body.

Then it's the Testosterone injections to give me weight gain, mood swings, hot flushes and generally let me know what the menopause feels like. Trust me, it was the worst sales pitch I've ever been given, but that or potentially more secondary cancers made it a relatively easy decision.

So to all my female friends of a certain age, I'm with you Sisters!!!

The only other hurdle to overcome is my Mo BillyT, yesterday saw some small green shoots of recovery. Today will deliver even more - So have a great day everyone from the People's Republic of Salford :)

Tug Gram 13

Unlucky for some, but given I arrived here having walked under a ladder, crossed the path of a black cat, and tripped over a broomstick that had been carelessly discarded, I shan't unduly concern myself that this is my 13th Tug Gram

Yesterday was awesome. I smashed my physio which concentrated on balance and maintaining centre of balance whilst swaying. Given I did 10 years in the Navy walking on decks that never stood still, re-establishing a centre of balance when swaying from side to side wasn't difficult. That said when I tried the same exercises two days previously, I was like the proverbial drunken sailor returning offshore after a 24-hour binge - so feel more confident than ever that I am on the home lap of this epic journey.

Today is my nuclear scan, when following the radioactive injection, I shall head into the bowels of Salford Royal glowing green like the kid on the ready-brek advert. I often wondered how they created those special effects when he was walking to school. Now I know! I just hope his parents took a big wedge of cash for making their child glow like a Chernobyl refugee.

More physio today, looking forward to it already, but somewhat hampered by a case of COVID on the ward, which means every member of staff enters the ward dressed like the Michelin man in full PPE. At least it gives me a soft landing should I fall. Enjoy your Friday people, from the depths of the Costa Del Salford :)

Emma, niece, on The Wilsons WhatsApp: Oh my gosh, he should so write a book! I don't read anything – it's actually a standing joke that Beck will often say she will get me the Kitty books as that's my limit but I could read Uncle Phil's books no problem. It's like my positive start to the day reading his messages xxx

Tug Gram 14

Day 24 in the Big Brother House, I would tell you what the weather is like but I haven't seen natural light since I arrived. Not been secured inside a space without natural light for so long since the Icelandic patrols on HMS Scylla in 1973.

It would appear my sojourn in the People's Republic of Salford is coming to an end with plans to move me to the Devonshire Centre in Stockport, which is a dedicated Neuro Rehab centre for a spot of intense physio to recover the use of my limbs and get me back, hopefully, to how I was before the tumour reshuffled the deck of cards. Given I joined the Navy in 1972 as a Devonshire Rating, feels like the right place to be.

Nuclear scan went well yesterday, albeit a painful experience to lay on my back on hard plastic for 45 minutes, but hopefully when the results arrive the discomfort will have been worth it. Not sure if I'll get physio today, but if it happens great, if not I may just have a lazy day and stay in :)

Tug Gram 15

In keeping with most Karen's on FB, I didn't want an extra hour of 2020, but I have to say that the extra hours sleep was most welcome. I slept from 10 pm until 6am, stirred occasionally but right back to sleep. So here I am fit (ish) and ready for what the world throws at me (Note to World, please don't take that literally and offer me more tumours and other cancers, I've really had enough of those if you don't mind)

Admittedly my sleep last night was Mo assisted, but welcome nonetheless. Still feeling the effects on my back from my scan on Friday, but given nothing happens on the ward today - not even the Jehovah's Witnesses (Occupational Health) come round on a Sunday, I should be able to rest.

So have a great Sunday everyone, enjoy what little fun has been left to enjoy in these lockdown times. As we say on the Costa Del Salford "ve a buscar gente", which for those who are not multilingual like wot I'm not, means (I'm assured) "Go get them People" :)

For the aficionados of these blogs, you will understand what I mean by my reference to the Jehovah's Witnesses (see Tug

Gram7). Anyway they will be round later distributing their equivalent of the watchtower and sorting out my transfer, wonder if they are getting a fee?

And YAY, should have a session of Physio :)

Double YAY, may get the results of the Nuclear Scan this week, so hopefully CND will stop marching with their banners at the end of my bed - and go back to Faslane (bit of political satire there). Suspect this will be my last week on the Costa del Salford. Can think of worse places to spend your vacation :)

Tug Gram 16

Happy Monday everyone. This is going to be the Mother of all weeks.

Have a great week everyone :)

Tug Gram 17

Day 27 in the Big Brother House. What surprises do we have in store today?

Our bay of 7 patients is now down to 4, after one patient was moved to ICU overnight (not Covid related).

Covid is having an effect though, my transfer to the Neuro Rehab hospital cannot take place until I've produced 2 negative tests. So 1 down, 1 to go. (I wonder if Liverpool lose in Europe tonight, that will count as a negative test?). Anyway it is what it is, and I shall transfer to the Rehab centre when I can. :)

Physio was very tough yesterday, walking up and down the ward between 2 nurses (that wasn't the tough bit, the two nurses, it was the walking), I'm sure they made the ward longer every time we turned at the end. That was followed by marching on the spot.

Anyway I'm expecting my knighthood anytime soon, as I walked as far as Captain Tom and he had a Zimmer frame, I just had 2 nurses and I'm sure I did all the work :)

More Physio today after I challenged them to exercise me every day (me and my big mouth!!!), but small price to pay if I'm to walk back into the piggy pub anytime soon :)

Still no sign of my Nuclear scan results, but I'm sure once they have something to tell me, they'll let me know.

Have a great day everyone.

Tug Gram 18

Day 28 in the Big Brother house. 4 weeks in this oasis of calm and tranquillity that is Salford Royal. 4 weeks ago today that I went to Romiley gym and tried to beat my best time for 0.5Km on the treadmill, now my success is measured by being supported as I walk (well walk may be a slight exaggeration, more like a very poor impression of a hop, skip & jump) 12 feet across the ward.

At least waking up this morning didn't feel like I was waking up in the middle of an Arthur Conan Doyle plot. For the last 3 mornings, I have woken up to another empty bed on the ward, another inmate mysteriously disappeared during the night. The only thing missing was the chalk outline of the body, and the detective in a deerstalker hat, smoking a pipe, and stating Elementary Dear Watson. They are trying to blame COVID isolation, but I know a good murder mystery when I see one.

Pain in my back prevented physio yesterday, but I am hopeful a bit of rest this morning will enable a physio session later. 2nd Covid test completed, should have results within 48 hours then my transfer will be scheduled.

Have a good day xx

Tug Gram 19

It is said that the only constant in life is change (and oh yeah death and taxes), but let's put them to one side for now

It would appear God has decided to give another shake of his dice and roll the Covid dice in my direction. So as of last night I am Covid positive and in 14-day isolation on a side ward. I am thinking of starting a sweepstake to see what gets me first;

1. *Cancer*

2. *Stroke*

3. *Boredom*

4. *Covid*

5. *Laxative overdose - can't take it anymore :)*

Answers on a postcard please.

The real downside is having started Physio, and enjoying it, I will lose all of that unless we are both in PPE. As we used to say in the Navy, a double bagger - As to what is going to happen to my transfer to a rehab centre, think it more likely I will be consigned to the International Space station - Anyway the next person who tells me they love my positivity, is going to get the Covid swab kit rammed up them sideways :)

So back to taxes. I wonder what the odds would have been to have a tumour, cancer and Covid within days of each other. I would have thought pretty good odds - Have a good day!!!

Becky, niece, on The Wilsons WhatsApp: Bad luck comes in three's – at least he's done!

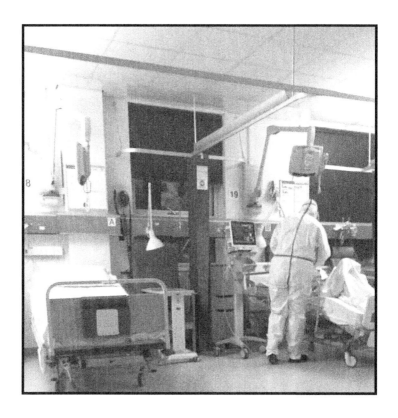

Casually, living a real-life scene from a pandemic movie like Outbreak or Contagion...

Tug Gram 20

This solitary confinement isn't all it's cracked up to be - just as well I like my own company.

Challenged the staff how I managed to catch Covid in an isolation ward when I was restricted to my own bed. They advise an investigation is taking place but it is likely that one individual who was able to go off the ward and even leave the hospital may have introduced the virus. The mind boggles! Anyway it is what it is, I'm also assured that my Covid status shouldn't prevent my being transferred to the rehab unit, so hopefully today is when all cases are reviewed by the combined medical teams, and following my review I should get firm plans announced. The very least I expect from my review is the fact I have run out of things to catch - Assuming they don't introduce leprosy or Ebola to the ward :)

Tug Gram 21

So the cell has not got any smaller overnight, although a decent night's sleep does make the outlook appear brighter. 1st November, so been incarcerated here for exactly 1 month, with no obvious exit plan in sight. The Multi-discipline team (MDT) reviewed my case file last week, and should be briefing me early next week. My request of them was very simple, feedback on the nuclear scan, and an effective exit strategy to enable me to enter a rehab facility, it would appear my next Covid swab is due on the 4th Nov., and I need to register 2 negative swabs to be considered for a transfer. So ever the *optimist, early November it is then. That assumes whatever the latest lockdown rules allow intra-hospital transfers. The whole scenario has the making of a total cluster-f**k.*

There appears to be an inordinate amount of hospital bed movements going on in the hospital, albeit I have a very limited view through the small door window in my room. So either there is a master plan in the process of execution in the hospital to redeploy patients, or the staff are bored out of their skulls, and playing some kind of go-karting game using hospital patients. Have a great Sunday everyone xx

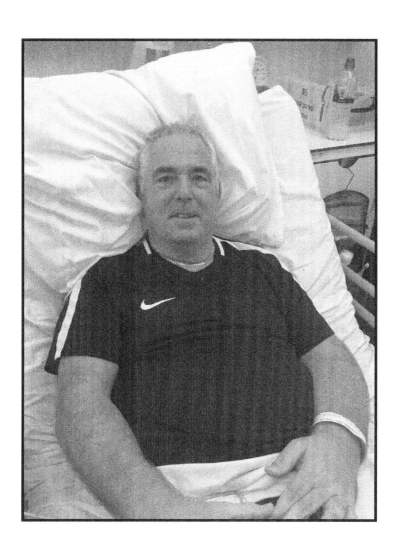

Another day in paradise!

Tug Gram 22

*Another fine night's sleep following a liberal dose of Mo Feen
:)*

*Am expecting the consultant today to finally give the outcome
of my nuclear scan, it is also suggested they will require
another, and hopefully, final scan, this time on my hip. I must
have the most photographed limbs on the planet, well after
the Royals, and maybe the Kardashians, and possibly Donald
Trump's wig :)*

*Been here for just over a month, and for the first time
managed to drop my urine bottle mid-use. Not a pleasant
experience, but at least it settled the debate "Shower or wash
at sink" - Shower it is then :)*

*2 more days until my Covid test YAY!!! Still no symptoms, so
have to be optimistic it's a negative!!!!*

Have a great week everyone :)

Tug Gram 23

*I'm advised my Covid test will take place today, and assuming
negative that will kick off the process to get me into rehab*

and eventually home. Still no clearer why the interest in my hip, but maybe as they say ignorance is bliss :)

Would appear they have closed the men's wards and repopulated with females, so not sure what happens or where I go if I am Covid negative. I assume a couple of hormone injections doesn't qualify me to reside in a women's ward.

I hope the Covid test also precipitates a return for the physio team, been a few days now. Luckily, I have been ignoring the stay in bed rule and walking to the ensuite toilet in my cell. Whatever happens, I am hoping for an eventful, interesting day xx :)

Tug Gram 24

Very much a mixed day yesterday, my Covid test did not take place and is scheduled for today, and even if the test is negative, I still have to spend a further 7 days in isolation. The issue with my hip was initially diagnosed as another cancer, but then reclassified as arthritis, so a real rollercoaster of emotion.

So I think I can definitely say yesterday was a bit of a wobble for me. Just coming up to 5 weeks in hospital and still no end in sight. I seriously thought of just signing myself out of hospital and taking my chances at home. Covid is playing havoc with my physio and potential rehab, and the isolation is getting harder each passing day.

Luckily the voice of reason that is Rob, Jenni & Ellen made me see the folly of such an action. Having done 7 days in isolation, I am halfway there, I can cope with another 7 days. The voices of reason and rationale were added to by the voices of my piss-taking x-Wren friends, Lucanne & Pat, who both made reference to my arthritis simply meant I was getting old - thanks ladies, kick a man whilst he is down why don't you!!! In truth however, just what I needed. It is too easy to fall into the trap of feeling sorry for yourself, and sometimes you need that dose of reality to refresh your thinking and refocus your mind.

So today is a new day. I am determined to renew my commitment to the bed exercises I have been given to strengthen my core and to push for more Physio if possible, and to see out this isolation time without further "wobbles" to allow my treatment to continue and get me back home.

So thank you to the voices of reason and for my piss-taking x-Wren buddies. You've helped me over a bump in the road, and I'm back on track. xxx

Lucanne, Friend and Navy veteran, on Messenger at my news and my despair: Oh for pity's sake, stop being a big girl's blouse.

This message, more than any, had me roaring with laughter, and it reminded me why my veteran friends are so important in my life. What made it even funnier was we confessed to each other afterwards that neither of us knew what 'A Big Girls Blouse' meant!

Tug Gram 25

Whilst Mo Billy T was the Barry White of the group, providing that deep tenor velvet voice so loved by his female fans, and Mo Feen provided the all-round support that held the group together, it was the backing singers Mo & Jo who gave the group harmony. When he had his Mo Jo back, anything was possible, he could take on the world :)

Hope to get the results of my Covid test today, but it doesn't matter, things will move at the pace they move. Mo Jo will see to that :)

Hope things move forward, but again it doesn't matter. Will continue to do my daily core exercises to strengthen mobility and just be ready to move to the next stage of this adventure when fate decrees it to be. I have faced lots of adversity in the past 5 weeks, another few days won't matter a jot. Stay safe everyone. Look forward to the day when all of this is just a postscript on that rich tapestry of our lives, and out stories begin, "Do you remember when..."

Enjoy your day people, live it to the fullest :)

Tug Gram 26

Day 38 in the Big Brother House, and today's bush-trucker trial comprises eating cold toast and drinking weak tea. What I wouldn't give for a decent cup of tea or coffee - Sill no sign of my Covid clearance, but what will be will be. I am sure it will come through and I will be transferred to the Devonshire Centre for neuro rehabilitation. Can't come soon enough, but no point in fretting on things outside of my control. Had a really bad night from a pain perspective last night, but then I effectively doubled up on my physio yesterday, so today is most definitely a rest day :)

Had more X-rays yesterday on my hip, hoping that is the last of the scans or I will be glowing in the dark :)

Really optimistic that today will see my Covid clearance come through and I will begin my recover journey back home. Thank you to everyone for their best wishes over the last 5+ weeks, it's been hard but you have seen me through this. Thank you xx

Tug Gram 27

Over 5 weeks since I entered the hallowed halls of Hogwarts, and I don't know about learning magic, but those magic mushrooms they use in the morphine certainly enable some special hallucinations - sadly I am still Covid positive, but I am sure it cannot be too long before I am given the all-clear, after all I have been in self isolation for 9 days without even a game of Quidditch with my fellow inmates.

Had a good physio session yesterday and for the first time since I arrived, I felt as my legs were actually doing what I asked them to do, albeit gingerly - I have to remember it's been a few weeks since they've been asked to take my weight and move on instruction so I should expect them to be a tad rusty.

The nursing staff are confident I will be Covid free soon, so they will re-swab me in a few days, and then I am sure I will be starting my homeward journey. Sadly unlike when I came back from Navy deployments, we shan't park up in the English Channel and drink industrial quantities of beer to let off steam before we were let loose on the UK population.

Have a fantastic weekend everyone, I think I may have a weekend in for a change and enjoy the lockdown - Welcome to my world :)

Tug Gram 28

This is worse than waiting for the results of Trump -v- Biden!!! Waiting for the results of my latest Covid swab. Like Trump though, if it doesn't go my way, I shall demand a recount - Assuming fortune favours the brave, then my results will be negative and I will transfer to the Devonshire Neuro Centre possibly today or tomorrow for more intense physio before being sent home. I shall bid Adieu to my cell and home for the past few weeks and begin a new chapter in this amazing adventure of Joseph and his Technicolor Dreams, admittedly mainly fuelled by morphine - As I recover from the spinal compression of my nervous system. Sounds dead easy if you sat it quickly, but I'm sure like physio in the past it will be painful, repetitive and I shall end up casting doubt on the parentage of those who are delivering my treatment :)

Tug Gram 29

Surely now, I can hear you thinking, he must be close to departure, and yes, I'm sure I am, but Salford Royal Spa & Sanatorium has thrown a couple of late spanners in the works to ease my passing.

On the positive front, my last swab came back Covid free YAY!!!!

However, Salford Spanner - I had not completed the 14-day mandatory isolation period, so in the wisdom of Salford Royal they decided I should spend the remaining 3 days of isolation in, of course, the Covid ward BOO!!!!

Many complaints from myself, Rob & Jenni later, they are moving me to a secure, non-Covid ward YAY!!!!

Because I've been in contact with Covid, I need to be swabbed clear again BOO!!!! My flabber is gasted that no-one saw this as a consequence of their decision!!!! They will fast track the swab, and ensure my place at the Devonshire Neuro Rehab centre is secure - Which means best news of all, the Tug Grams really are drawing to a close.

Jacqui, sister, on The Wilsons WhatsApp: OMFG what a farce!

Tug Gram 30

Jenni, daughter, on The Wilsons WhatsApp: Here we go, today's war and peace.

Well I'm now safely ensconced in my new home, which is effectively just a different view of the Costa Del Salford, but nevertheless some distance from Covid City - It appears I shall undergo physio whilst on this ward and the team are neuro-physio trained, rather than the generalists in the previous ward, so hopefully they will be able to help me rather than just cause me pain.

It transpires an official investigation has been instigated by my consultant as to how I was incarcerated on the Covid ward, and whilst I am just pleased to be off the ward and to be somewhere safe it is probably right that the events are analysed to prevent a reoccurrence. I should pay tribute to Jenni and Rob for their support in getting me off the Covid ward, especially Jenni who seemed to have raised mayhem in every part of Salford on my behalf.

I shall also hopefully find out today if I still have my place at the Devonshire Neuro Rehab unit, and when I will actually transfer the short distance from Salford to Offerton to begin rehab work. I am really looking forward to it, I feel my body is ready to start working again, it just needs to be shown how to.

I have to say the staff here are very attentive when they get to you, but they do tend to ignore the call button, so I just hope I don't have an emergency, because I suspect I will just get a response like something out of Coronation Street "What ye doing down there Chuck? And what's all that red stuff you're spilling everywhere, look at the mess you're making. Stanley, get him up, he's clashing with my Muriel"

Today would have been my mum's birthday, so all the best mater on whichever cloud you're resident on, probably berating a saint or two somewhere. For all of her faults, and trust me there were many, she did not do a bad job of bringing up 10 kids. All of whom have not made a bad fist of their own lives.

For the first time in a few days I am truly optimistic for the future, Physio are about to launch themselves on me like in the opening sequence from Gladiator "Release the Hounds of Hell, Maximus Decimus Meridius"

Bring it on, and have a great day everyone from a sunny Costa del Salford. xx

Tug Gram 31

Star date 11th November 2020. A somewhat apt date for what I hope is the final part of my epic journey. Hopefully this will be my last Tug Gram from the Peoples Republic of Salford, I should transfer to Her Britannic Majesty's Dependency of

Offerton later today to begin Neuro rehabilitation which should, with a fair wind and full sail, allow me to get home.

Salford has been different. They are very keen on preventing issues from long term bed rest such as bed sores, so they give you an assessment twice a day to ensure no adverse conditions have occurred since the last inspection. The concept is admirable, but the execution by a couple of Salford based, Glaswegian middle-aged female nurses, giving commentary like "Oh Jules, this is a right peach, just feel how firm it is" or "Nice legs, he can chase after me any day" are not what you expect at 5.30 in the morning.

That said it's quite good for the ego, I might book them for morning visits when I get home :)

I can't believe it's exactly 6 weeks since this adventure began. Let's just hope that whichever Deity decides the direction our lives take is bored with me, and allows me to settle down for a while with no further "episodes or excitement"

For me the next few weeks will be dedicated to recovering my health and mobility. By recovering my mobility I may repay in a small way the love and support I have received from Rob & Jenni and so many other people over this period. I will not let you down, I shall walk back into the Piggy and order a pint as soon as lockdown allows :)

This is the first day of the rest of my life :)

Tug Gram 32

Greetings from paradise - Well I'm finally here in the opulent oasis of her Britannic Majesty in Offerton. Such a remote outpost of the empire that even Attila the Hun and his hordes were too afraid to invade, so swerved round it and headed straight to Londonium.

It is exactly as I remember it from my time here as an outpatient after my stroke. It has a very calm, relaxing atmosphere, but one that feels efficient and purposeful. What was really nice was a couple of the staff recognized Elaine from the photograph I have of her on my shelf, and they asked after her. Elaine used to bring me here the last time I used the facility, and you will not be surprised to know, she used to talk to everyone :)

I'm already booked in for my first occupational and Physio assessments this afternoon, and really looking forward to them and for making progress in my recovery. I know I need to set myself realistic expectations, but I have such a positive feeling about this place.

The Bamboo nightclub in Offerton may be long gone, but the spirit and resilience of the people remain.

I will be realistic, but I am already envisaging myself at home - Wish me luck xx

Tony, brother, on The Wilsons WhatsApp: Here is rooting for you Phil. Keep the spirits up – not the alcohol.

Happy Tug Gram 33

Woke this morning to a feeling I have not had for a long time, aching muscles. Muscles reminding you that you are making them do things they are not used to, and I can't tell you how wonderful it felt. I know I am using muscles that have lain dormant for weeks, and I may suffer later, but I don't care, the pain is more than worthwhile.

So my first 24 hours here at the Devonshire, and it is everything I expected. Their Raison D'etre is entirely focused on getting me into the best physical and emotional condition to prosper on my own without close support. The entire staff have bubbly northern personalities, in fact I think it must be part of their recruitment criteria that they all have a dirty laugh, it would be incredibly difficult to be depressed in here - I can't think the last time I felt so positive in my outlook, but that is a feature of the Devonshire. I am already looking forward to my physio, and am so optimistic they will make a difference for me.

I shan't fall into the trap of thinking about how long it will be when I will get home, I shall simply focus on the daily physio and trust in their judgement that I will get home when I'm ready.

More staff have commented on Elaine's photograph. They all seem to remember her, but no-one seems to recall me from my time here as an outpatient. That says so much about Elaine and her personality, and makes me even more determined to recover as best I can, for Elaine, but also for Rob & Jenni (make sure they don't have access to their inheritance until I'm good and ready)

Friday 13th, but I feel anything but unlucky. Have a great day everyone xx

Happy Tug Gram 34

OMG how civilised is this place, we get a lie-in at the weekend with tea and toast not served until 8am :)

Still feeling the euphoria from my first steps yesterday, and even though there is no physio at weekends I know I shall practise my standing from my chair and walking across the room before returning to my chair and sitting down again. Don't know which is the greater challenge, the 10 sit to stand repetitions set by the physiotherapist or the "How many steps you done today Grandad" from Olivia? Woe betide me if I can only come up with a feeble excuse like "No steps today Oli, they were operating on my spine". She simply doubles the number of steps required for me to do the following day :)

I really cannot work out why this place radiates positivity, but it does. You can't help but feel hopeful and optimistic being here, whether it is because the staff all smile and have that Northern way of talking to everyone, or whether it is simply the right time in my recovery treatment to feel this way and want to improve. Whatever the reason I feel very confident I will make a reasonable recovery from the spinal surgery.

I appreciate you are in the midst of a lockdown, nevertheless make the most of your weekend and enjoy each other's company. Live your weekend to the full. xxx

Jacqui, sister, on The Wilsons WhatsApp: What a gorgeous message. I'm loving Phil's renewed confidence and positivity.

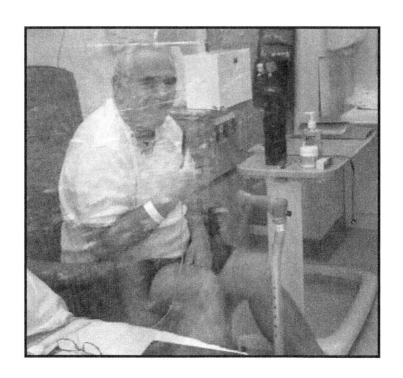

A screenshot from a video recorded through the window on the hospital ward when Jenni came to visit. In it, I'm heard saying, "Wish you were here – instead of me!"

Jenni, daughter, on The Wilsons WhatsApp: Dad thinks he's hilarious.

Claire, sister, on The Wilsons WhatsApp: :/

Holly, niece, on The Wilsons WhatsApp: Hahaha :/

Becky, niece, on The Wilsons WhatsApp: He is to be fair :/

Emma, niece, on The Wilsons WhatsApp: Hahaha

Nicola, niece, on The Wilsons WhatsApp: :/

Jacqui, sister, on The Wilsons WhatsApp: Lovely to see you Phil. Looking good! :/

Happy Tug Gram 35

My first Sunday in the Devonshire Centre, and in the nicest possible way, I hope I shan't spend too many more Sundays in here, but they certainly like Sundays to be relaxed.

Still getting over the shock and delight of seeing Rob & Jenni when they visited me yesterday. A total surprise and after 7 weeks without seeing friends or family, a pleasure beyond description. To add to the pleasure we then had a FT call with Olivia & Sara playing at my house, and again the first time I had seen the inside of my house for 7 weeks. So an emotional experience, but certainly not one to complain about. Of course first question from Olivia on the FT call was "how many steps today Grandad?". She didn't appear impressed with my response that I am practicing "Sit to Stand" not steps, it was "yeah, but how many steps" What a slave driver :)

Looking forward to a restful day, before really going at the physio next week. From the Oasis that is Offerton, Enjoy your Sunday xx

Happy Tug Gram 36

First working day of the new week, and it already feels special. Yesterday Rob brought his wife Ellen and two granddaughters Olivia & Sara to see me in the hospital. It was lovely to see everyone after such a long time in isolation, and I was right that the first question from slave-driver Olivia was "how many steps Grandad". It was no excuse that I was in a wheelchair :)

I am really optimistic that by the end of this week, I should have some idea of how long it will be before I'm allowed home. I shall remain realistic, I know there are still a few challenges remaining, but I do feel I am making progress and am really confident the Therapy teams will push me hard to get me ready to go home.

I completed my 20 repetitions of sit to stand yesterday, but thought I would add a twist and position my wheelchair one side of the room, and my easy chair the other side. I would stand from one chair, walk the 7 steps to the wheelchair then sit down, which meant I had to complete 10 circuits to meet my target. I swear this room was like something out of Harry Potter, and it got wider the more repetitions I completed. By the last circuit I felt like I was circumnavigating the M25 the distance between chairs was so great, but I finished it :)

Not sure what occupational and physio therapies I have today, but I know I will push myself and get the most from the sessions. Have a great week as I enjoy the wonders and delights from the Royal dependency of Offerton.

Happy Tug Gram 37

Physio is going well as I look to build up strength on my weak side and regain functionality lost after the spinal compression from the tumour. It is painful, but I am enjoying the challenge and look forward to today's agonizing fun & games :)

It is also a period where attention refocuses on the cancer. So today I have the 2nd of my hormone injections to reduce testosterone levels - I wonder if it comes with a free gift like you used to get with "Woman's Own", free mascara and lipstick with every injection? Or maybe 50% reduction when you book your next perm with every injection!!!

Then tomorrow my first visit to the oncology specialist at Christie's. I just hope they take me to the right place; I mean I know I'm putting on the years, but I would hate to be sold at Christie's auction house as an antique, especially if I didn't make my reserve :)

Hopefully though I shall find out some details about the cancer and if I got it as a try before you buy version - send it back if it doesn't suit within 90 days - I'm sure the medical teams have explained my cancer before now, but unfortunately every time they have tried, I've been floating above the ionosphere high on morphine each time an explanation has been offered, so I probably thought they were talking about birth signs and I'd have been going "No, I'm Aries, not Cancer."

Here's looking forward to another fabulous day in my fight to recover and get back home, if only to make sure that Angie's mum hasn't supped all of the brandy. Have fun everyone, from an Opulent Offerton x

Happy Tug Gram 38

Well here I am at Oncology, should be a fun session, hearing for the first time about my cancer without the protective barrier of Morphine. May actually realise what I have :)

When I was on HMS Eskimo, our standard routine when coming back offshore was to get on our knees and walk back to the ship in single file on our knees singing "Hi Ho Hi Ho, to the Eskimo we go". All morning I have not been able to get "Hi Ho Hi Ho, to Oncology we go" out of my head. I just hope I'm not thinking it aloud or it may be a quick transfer from Oncology to Strait Jacket :)

Have my list of questions for the Doctor, but deleted my first question, which was "why me?" Just in case I didn't like the answer, if it was something like "Don't take it personally, we give this to all Scousers" :)

Looking forward to another workout with the physios today, no doubt more step ups. Once I'm out of here I shall avoid steps like the plague unless I absolutely must use them, like when there is a step to get to the bar or something equally critical :)

Tug Gram 39

I reckon my first consideration today is for my first born, Rob, who is 38 years old today. Elaine would be, as indeed I am, immensely proud of what Rob & Jenni have achieved with their lives. They have both become two of the most grounded, decent people you could ask for. We couldn't ask for better children, thank you.

Another day in the magnificent opulence of Offerton, I think I can safely say I will get more physio, which translates to more pain, but hey ho, they've got to get their fun somehow

The meeting yesterday with the oncologist did not go as planned, to say I came away understanding less than when I arrived is an understatement. I think my cancer comprises of big, unpronounceable words that are impossible to remember. Someone needs to produce a series of books, starting with "Prostate Cancer for Dummies", then I may have a chance of understanding my condition. Have a great day peoples, live today as best you can, and enjoy every moment.

Tug Gram 40

A much more informed day yesterday, got more insight about my cancer from the consultant's office, and more information on how it will be treated. Started with a new drug regime which supports the hormone suppressant monthly injection in stopping Testosterone circulate the cancer and spread the cancer around the body. This means stories of my demise have been greatly exaggerated, and I may even be around to watch Liverpool win the Premiership again, although I'll likely be 95 years old so I may struggle to see the screen. I was also told to carefully read the possible side effects, which I did. Didn't want to risk that well known side effect "May start to support Man United" or "May start to feel sympathy for Everton". Anyway it appears I'm safe from both conditions for now. I also start Radiotherapy later in November, which is not something I came across as a Royal Navy Radio Operator, but assume it's like Morse Code with a bit of a kick.

Also started a new exercise regime that I can do whilst lay on my bed and is intended to strengthen my legs. The concept is great, but given the exercises require me to bend my knees and hold them in position on bedding that is like lying on the Antarctic ice shelf, my legs end up slipping out of position faster than a sprinter on performance enhancing acid.

Getting towards the end of another week, and whilst my bed exercises may not be successful yet, overall my daily physio is making a difference and I am getting stronger and walking further. Not far enough for Olivia though, yesterday I proudly announced I had walked 250 steps, and quick as a flash (which also reflects well on her mathematics), Olivia said "well tomorrow you should do 500 steps" The challenge is on!

Tug Gram 41

Here we are at another civilised Saturday in Sunny (not) Stockport. Was going to go sunbathing, but I believe the sun *loungers have been put away, and we only have factor -40 sun cream. Apparently stops the sun but not frostbite.*

I failed in my challenge yesterday, got nowhere near 500 steps, but mainly because the OT's concentrated on my arm movements. If you think I would struggle to walk 500 steps with my feet, you can bet I wouldn't do it on my hands, even after an hour's manipulation of my arm and shoulder.

I shall just have to change the subject if Olivia raises the matter, get her talking about the solar system, an area of expertise for Olivia (I kid you not) or discussing the latest antics of Peppa Pig (an area of expertise for Olivia and Sara) Woe betide you if you ever make the mistake of coming between the TV with Peppa Pig playing and Sara. As they say "Hell hath no fury like a baby-woman interrupted during Peppa Pig"

Even though weekends are rest days with no physio, I have managed to volunteer for 2 hours of OT and Physio today and tomorrow. I knew I should have listened to the Recruiting Petty Officer when he told me "Never volunteer", but hopefully the extra physio will pay off and my limbs will regain a bit more strength.

Been 48 hours now without my mate and mentor, Mo Feen, and I can honestly say the pain has been negligible. Bit of a niggle when I'm doing physio, but if I rest after it soon eases. Hopefully this means the back wound is getting close to being fully healed, or that I have lost all feeling in my back. Think I'll opt for the back healed option.

Tug Gram 42

Radiotherapy is now locked and loaded for the 27th November, by the description given to me it will just be like going on an episode of the Golden Shot, (google it if you are not of a certain age). I just hope they don't invite TV contestants to fire the radio beam at my spine in an effort to win a prize.

Also been considering the advice of the consultant that I need to be body aware and remain vigilant of any new and developing tumours, but in truth the advice is like a hypochondriac's charter. I think I've already had over 300 new tumours in my legs until I'm able to rationalise that the pain niggles are from physio. The definite tumour in my mouth turned out to be a rogue piece of lettuce from my Turkey salad stuck to the inside of my gum, and the new swelling found on my thigh was established on closer investigation to be a forgotten lump of putty that they use to exercise my hands and strengthen my fingers. Tiring work this "Medical Watch", just as well I am not working this week.

I keep checking my moobs to see if they are getting bigger, but so far not.

Even though it's Sunday, I've elected to do another hour of physio today. I know a martyr to the cause :)

Finished joint last in the family quiz last night. It was a really good quiz thanks Jenni. If only I could have had a point for every question mark I wrote to indicate I didn't have a clue to the answer, I would have romped home :)

Enjoy your Sunday everyone :)

Rob, son, on The Wilsons WhatsApp: Joint last?! He came last last!

Tug Gram 43

Another week luxuriating in the Opulence of Offerton, enjoying the delights and delicacies that can only be found in a Northern town. Tripe, belly-pork, and of course gravy on everything, including dessert :)

This is also the week that the Devonshire Centre will conclude its assessment of if, and when, I will be able to return home based on my ability to mobilise and look after myself. Now we'll see if that extra physio has paid off. I will try to maintain a balanced view on whatever decision is reached. I am pretty sure I will be able to go home at some point, it is whether my limbs have regained sufficient use to determine if it is now, or maybe in another couple of weeks. I shall take the view that whatever the choice, it will have been made with my interests at the heart of it, so I should respect the conclusion reached.

And anyway life isn't all bad, Liverpool won again - against the odds given their injury list, which is longer than the time it is taking President Trump to concede defeat in the presidential race with Biden. The food is okay, and Lockdown ensures I am not missing out on anything.

So here's to another great week, enjoy your time whether working or leisure, and remember the words of that great philosopher Confucius. "Wheresoever you go, go with all your heart", or was it that naval quote? "It is better to be p*ssed off, than p*ssed on". I leave you to judge

Tug Gram 44

Tomorrow will mark my 8th week of incarceration, a term normally reserved for relatively minor misdemeanours such as shop-lifting, traffic offences or low-level drug trafficking (maybe I should blame my mate Mo Feen). Talking of whom, today will be the 6th day since Mo Feen went AWOL (Absent without Leave for the non-military types amongst us). I am pleased to say his absence has not been noticed and my back pain is now totally under control, which is a major step forward. Equally rewarding is that both of his mates, the rappers Mo Billy T and Mo Shun have stepped up to the plate in Mo Feen's absence and made their presence known. So I now appear to be able to walk for short distances, albeit with the aid of a stick, without looking like a sailor coming back offshore after a 24-hour bender. Not that I would know what that looks like. My balance is improving as each day passes, so I no longer look like a rocking horse on amphetamines. All of which means my ability to return home now has a greater chance of reality. I don't believe it will be reviewed until after my radiotherapy this coming Friday, but am hopeful that a date will be set shortly thereafter. At this point I would normally announce my imminent return with the warning to lock up your womenfolk, but with the drug regime heavily weighted towards testosterone suppression this may no longer be necessary. :)

Have a great day :)

Tug Gram 45

So all change on the ward last night, another couple of new entries, one of whom requires 24-hour supervision so for ease I moved into the main ward (of 6 beds, but only 3 occupied), not a problem for me as long as it doesn't disrupt my physio. Because the REAL big news is I have my estimated discharge date, which is the 22nd December. The Physio staff believe on my current trajectory I could shave a week off this date, but I will be realistic and aim for the 22nd. I am confident I can meet the earlier date, but I also recognise that I did a lot of physio yesterday and my legs are extremely painful today, which is fine, I will exercise through that pain, but it is a timely reminder that I still need to rebuild strength and stamina. So optimistic, but realistic. I have to remain cognisant that I am coming off the back of a major operation and serious illness, so all I can do is continue to work hard and aim for the earliest date, but accept the date that offers me the safest return home, and my reunion with my bottle of Red :)

Have fun everyone :)

Emma, niece, on The Wilsons WhatsApp: That's awesome xxx

Tug Gram 46

Another ward change last night, the staff are concerned that leaving me in a multi-bay ward puts me at greater risk of infection, so I have been moved to another side ward. Ensuite, and bigger, so more walking!!!!

Another day of physio, with the focus remaining on using my legs to step up. Part of me thinks, "WTF, I'm in a Bungalow", but I recognise that the 'step-up' is one of, if not the most difficult manoeuvre you get to perform with recalcitrant legs. Crack this, and much more follows, so step ups it is.

Radiotherapy tomorrow, can't fault the pace that things are moving at, just up to me to do my bit and get myself home in a fit(ish) state :)

Can't believe it's been 9 weeks since I booked into the Costa Del Salford hotel, a lot of water has passed under the bridge in that time, and whilst I wouldn't have taken this path by choice, at least it seems to be heading in a generally decent direction. :)

Tug Gram 47

So today is Radiotherapy Day.

I was going to google the procedure to see what it entailed, but then I thought it must be similar to Laser Quest, that indoor game facility where you strap on chest receivers and run around shooting each other with laser guns like a demented group of Special Forces teenagers. I took Rob to Laser Quest for one of his birthdays with a bunch of his mates, so it will be the same, just less fun.

Not that it was fun for me, I made the mistake of wearing a light-coloured cable-knit jumper for the game, a jumper which once inside and under the neon lights glowed like a "come and shoot me target" which meant of the 60 minutes you are inside the facility, I spent 58 of those minutes with disabled equipment as every time someone registers a 'hit' on your receiver, it is disabled for 90 seconds. Gives you some idea how many times, Rob and his freaking mates shot me during the hour :)

I shan't be caught out today though!!! I will be going to Christie's dressed in black from top to bottom with tiger-striped camouflage cream on my face. I will look like the Milk-tray man, sans the chocolates. They won't know what's hit them.

Have a great day everyone, I am sure I will have more to tell you once I have been "cooked" later today :)

Enjoy :)

Tug Gram 48

I feel that I continue to make good progress with Physio, walked over 400 metres yesterday, albeit with a stick, so not quite up to the pre-tumour standard of a daily 1Km+, but I'm happy with the way things are going and still believe I am on track for a 15th December homecoming as long as next Fridays cookery lesson doesn't deflect us. Still spending most of my physio session walking up and down steps, which is incredibly difficult, I just hope the tumour appreciates the efforts I am making to get him home for Christmas :)

As for the aforementioned cookery lesson. Radiotherapy begins next Friday 4th December, before a break for the weekend. Probably to allow it to be featured on Saturday Kitchen, "Tumour Au Gratin", not sure what vegetables should accompany the dish, but must ensure because we are Northern that Gravy is on the recipe :)

Radiotherapy then recommences Monday through Thursday 7th-10th December, so bad news for anyone who wanted "rare or medium rare" - Based on my experience yesterday, I will still be expected to complete physio, so it will be a competition to see which one tires me the most. Physio or Radiotherapy. Maybe a sweepstake is called for :)

Lie-in today, breakfast won't be served until 0830 and no Physio until Monday. I shall, however, have a sneaky personal physio session before my shower just to remind my legs what is expected of them, and I shall walk to the shower which is a good distance down the other end of the building (in the West

Wing I think they call it). No rest for the wicked, we still have a homecoming target to meet :)

Enjoy your weekend, as much as you can in whatever Tier you are living under. Just think of me in Tier 4 - No meeting with anyone indoors or outdoors, and no social activity unless it is Physio and it hurts.

Tug Gram 49

Just having a slice of toast and a cup of tea before I do a spot of Physio then will relax for the rest of Sunday. One more day of November before we enter the last month of 2020, a year I shall not be sorry to see the back of when we say Hi to 2021.

No idea what the Chinese symbol was for 2020, don't think it matters, it will always be the Year of the Bat. If I thought 2019 was a year to be best forgotten, 2020 left it dead in the water.

A spot of Physio will help to reset my priorities and remind me what is important, which is of course for me to get back home. Thought I was doing well by setting a new distance with my walking yesterday, until I got a post last night to say my daughter Jenni was 56 miles into an overnight 100-mile endurance race. Put my 400 meters into the shade. :)

Well done Jen :)

Enjoy the rest of your weekend folks. :)

Tug Gram 50

As I bring up my half-century of posts, I can't help but reflect on what the last 50 or so days has been like. From the initial thoughts and fears that I had had another stroke, to meeting my latest partner in crime - my tumour :)

It's been a hell of a ride and not one I would choose to repeat, but I've met some fantastic human beings in our NHS and had a great tour of Northwest medical establishments and wards. Today I feel like you do at the end of a holiday, had a great time, but ready to go home now :)

Going to give this tumour what for at Physio today, will really push hard as we reach the end of November to ensure I am able to return home in December. Hopefully leaving my barbecued crisp and crinkly tumour behind after radiotherapy this week and next :)

Definitely going to be a good week for me, I hope your week is equally good. :)

Tug Gram 51

Never thought I would be glad to feel the return of Spasticity (the pain you get from limbs as unused and previously redundant muscles are reawakened), but after yesterday's physio session which comprised of climbing up and down more stairs since before they found the tumour, and walking a greater distance - Spasticity is back - I know I should have taken it easy yesterday, but after Jenni's epic 100 mile run over the weekend, the only answer to "can you do a few more" was a resounding YES. Me and my big mouth - It did feel good though!!!

Family gets the chance to hear first-hand how I am progressing when we have a case conference tomorrow with the medical and therapy teams who will answer questions on my condition. It will be like Prime Ministers Questions in Parliament, but without the braying of opposition MP's (unless Rob or Jenni dislikes the answer) and hopefully no long-winded answers from the PM that says absolutely nothing. Obviously, the key question from the family will be when can we get our inheritance? At this point, a long-winded answer that says nothing is perfectly acceptable :)

The week is going to plan, Physio, more physio and in case I forget, a bit more physio - hope your week is equally productive :)

Tug Gram 52

Spent the night dreaming of the Family case review today, it's going to be a total role reversal similar to Parents evening, but with the children listening to an appraisal of the parents progress.

"Philip can be disruptive on the ward."

"If he doesn't enjoy the exercise, doesn't always put the effort in."

(Very true, hate the Occupational Health obsession with Play-Doh as a means of improving hand dexterity.)

"Sometimes talks during ward rounds."

"Distracts the other patients."

"His cancer is louder than the other cancers on the ward."

In reality parents evenings with Rob & Jenni were always occasions of immense pride, I cannot recall a single moment of criticism for either of them throughout their schooldays. Will I live up to the family tradition?

As long as it concludes with a discharge plan, I'll be content :)

Smashed Physio again yesterday, did even more stairs than ever before, did 4 walks of 100 metres, and also 4 or 5 x 15 metre walks over different surface types to challenge balance and footing. Great fun, even if at times I rolled and corrected myself like a Frigate in a force 10 Gale - And then went to the kitchen to demonstrate I could remain upright whilst making a cup of tea and toast. Smashed it!!! And it was a nice cup of tea which I got to drink before walking back to my ward.

Last big challenge will be the Radiotherapy starting Friday, here's hoping that doesn't set me back and I remain on track for discharge on or earlier than 22nd December. Have a great day everyone :)

Becky, niece, on The Wilsons WhatsApp: Everything crossed! xx

Tug Gram 53

Well Parents evening successfully navigated, the kids failed to convince the staff here to keep me in indefinitely - so still on track for departure late December. It was agreed that from a Physio perspective I could be ready to go home before the 22nd, but the question mark that is raised by my nemesis - radiotherapy - may yet necessitate further delays. My physical reaction to the barbecue of the tumour that is radiotherapy remains an unknown, so everyone is reserving judgement.

Nevertheless another good day of physio, beat my daily stair climb again. Was excused from walking on the different surface exercise as my balance remains a concern, and they will test that more over the next few days. So if you see me walking around with a book on my head, well my kindle, because I don't use actual books anymore, you'll know what I'm doing. If I'm lucky they will go the whole hog and make me drink a glass of wine whilst I'm walking with the kindle on my head :)

More physio today before the barbecue starts tomorrow. Enjoy your day :)

Tug Gram 54

Yesterday saw the 1st of my 5 radiotherapy sessions completed at Christie's, and I have to confess the actual process was painless and fairly straightforward. Although aligning my body for the lasers less so. Two technicians spent ages moving my body into position, millimetre by millimetre, like some mystical solstice celebration at Stonehenge when I had to be perfectly aligned with the stars.

Finally I was aligned, took about 15 minutes, then they ask you to stay perfectly still!! All was good until Rachel, one of the Technicians, placed her freezing cold hand on my chest as they were leaving to reassure me. I flinched from the cold and they had to start all over again. The same thing happened on the second attempt even though Rachel had rubbed her hands together to warm them before offering reassurances, so on the third attempt she simply waved her reassurances from the doorway before they retired behind the lead screens to activate the lasers.

I was wrong in my earlier posts, it wasn't like Laser Quest, more like the film set of Star Wars, with the Starfighters circling round the enemy (Me), firing their lasers intermittently. The actual treatment is very quick using state of the art technology, but I wasn't impressed with the audio tone of the laser. The monotone reminded me of the original boring Nokia Ringtone on mobiles. Surely this 21st Century set-up could have provided a choice of laser accompaniment sounds like on current mobile phones. That way, as part of treatment set-up, the patient selects their preferred laser tone. I'd have opted for "Ride of the Valkyries" by Wagner, much more appropriate when being zapped by starfighters :)

The whole treatment probably lasts 45 minutes, a proportion of that the caveats for what may occur post treatment. Luckily, I didn't experience the sickness they warned of, but I did welcome back some backache and felt incredibly tired. The tiredness surprised me because I just lay on the treatment table doing nothing, the Technicians even move your body into position, so I didn't get the tiredness at all. Nevertheless went to bed exhausted at 6 pm last night, and hardly slept a wink because my back and limbs were aching.

The biggest impact for me were the Wibbly-Wobbly arms and legs. I tried to walk to the toilet when I got back on the ward, and was like some cartoon character flapping across the ward. Pleased to say my legs seem to have recovered some firmness this morning, but I've yet tried to use them, so watch this space.

Back to Christie's on Monday for Part Deux. I just hope the weekend break is so they can demonstrate cooking the Tumour on Saturday Kitchen, and that they remember we are Northern, so just the juice from the Tumour and some Bisto. None of that fancy Southern tosh like "Tumour a L'Orange" :)

Have a great weekend folks :)

Tug Gram 55

So today is the weekly weigh-in day, and if it follows the same path as the previous 10 weeks, I shall lose a couple of Lb's. I have lost over a stone in weight since I was admitted to Salford Royal on 1st October. Better still the loss wasn't the drastic weight loss normally associated with cancer patients, rather a steady loss every week. So steady I am thinking of taking out a patent for my diet as a rival to the Atkins or LowCarb Diets, and indeed as a competitor to Weight Watchers. I admit that the brand name "Prostate Diet" may be seen as an extreme way to lose weight, and I'm not even sure that women are affected by this particular cancer so may not need to register "Prostates Diet" on my Patent. Nevertheless worthy of consideration. I accept there are downsides to the diet, predominantly the fact it could kill you, but as they say "no pain, no gain". :)

The treatment also has other downsides, I am already searching Amazon for a 3-cup Bra to accommodate my new Moobs and growing pot-belly that despite losing weight and with no alcohol for over 10 weeks appears to be a side-effect of the drug regime to manage the cancer. At least I assume the pot-belly is a side effect from the drug regime, with my luck it could evolve into my belly exploding and a tumour bursting out like in the film Alien, shouting "Honey I'm Home"

Unfortunately, or fortunately, depending on your viewpoint my Oppo Mo Feen is back supporting me as the effects of the radiotherapy become more apparent. So a rest day today before back to Christie's tomorrow which means the Tug Grams may be a bit erratic this week.

Normal service will be resumed as soon as possible :)

Tug Gram 56

Today is the halfway point in the radiotherapy treatment, with session 3 of 5 scheduled for this morning? The radiotherapy itself continues to be a painless process, but like all good Star Wars films, each time it delivers enigmatic aftereffects. In my episode "The Tumour fights back", the tumour reminds me of his omnipotence, a bit like Darth Vader, with bouts of backache and spasticity. Apparently the 5 treatments are intended to shrink and finally eradicate the tumour, and also stop any new growths. At the end of the 5 days I assume the tumour looks similar to one of those heads you see exhibited in museums and so beloved by the tribes in the Northwest Amazon. Maybe after the radiotherapy I should offer my Tumour to the British Museum as an exhibit :)

They did warn me that I might experience a bit of pain for a period during and after the radiotherapy, but this should ease within 14 days after treatment. They don't rescan to see the effect of the radiotherapy because they believe the recipient will be able to measure effectiveness by reductions in pain and improved mobility. Until then Mo Feen has re-joined as my best mate. Anyway onwards and upwards, Christie's won't start without me, so better start getting ready for today's laser war :)

Have fun xxx

Tug Gram 57

Final radiotherapy session today so with luck the tumour is now a black & crinkly shadow of its former self, hanging onto my spine by his fingertips, looking like the last sausage on the BBQ. The one that even the dog turns his nose up at.

I have to confess I have been surprised at the impact on me of the radiotherapy, especially when I consider on the outside it looks like such a benign solution to a major condition. Nevertheless that benign appearance belies a treatment which leaves you exhausted, moreover an exhaustion that isn't resolved with sleep. I can have a restful 6 hours sleep after a session of radiotherapy and still wake up tired - The treatment also leaves your limbs feeling weaker, so physio has been parked for the week. The Physiotherapists worried I may fall and seriously hurt myself when weakened after treatment (though I'm not sure I can be more seriously hurt than with cancer) I am gutted that I've missed physio, but think they are right, and accept that because of this I must wave goodbye to any aspirations of a discharge on the 15th December. Hopefully if I rest this weekend and blast the life out of physio next week, the 22nd remains an achievable date for discharge, but in any instance, I will be guided by the medics and go home when they say it's safe for me to do so :)

On a much more positive note, with due apologies to friends on FB who have already seen this news. 6 years ago, our daughter Jenni commenced an epic journey to her Doctorate. Elaine and I promised Jenni a holiday of her choice when she successfully completed the course. (That she would be successful was never in doubt), Jen chose Everest. Now going round a Double-glazing firm would not be my idea of a good day out, but each to their own. It was only later when we realised she actually wanted to climb that little hill in Nepal, I thought I won't get much change out of a tenner if she does that. Even though Elaine won't be here to see Jenni's success, I know she will be as proud as I will be when Jenni climbs Everest - though knowing Jenni, she will climb Everest walking backwards, carry a 60 Kg kitbag. :)

Stand at the summit Doctor Wilson - Doctor of Elite Performance - you're closer to your mum, enjoy the experience and allow our pride to wash over you :)

So radiotherapy nearly behind me, physio back on the horizon, what could possibly go wrong. Enjoy your day peeps, and have a great weekend in whatever Tier you find yourself in.

Jacqui, sister, on The Wilsons WhatsApp: Wow Phil, you're amazing. And congratulations again Jen. You're awesome xxx

Tug Gram 58

Can't believe I am entering my 11th week as a guest of Her Majesty's Hospitals, hopefully the end of this phase is in sight and I shall be home before too long when the real recovery starts. I have met some fantastic people during my tenure in Hospital, such warm, caring, compassionate and genuinely empathetic people, we are truly blessed with our NHS here in the UK. Nevertheless with good fortune and a fair wind I shan't have to test its effectiveness for much longer :)

I should also acknowledge that the messages of goodwill from my friends and family have been very much appreciated during my hospitalization. Messages from friends and old shipmates from around the UK and indeed around the world have helped tremendously, especially in those rare, dark moments when doubts about my future mobility crept into the foreground of my mind.

My children have been a constant source of support and inspiration, and I will feel very special having access to my own Doctor. I am so looking forward to the day I beg for help only to be told "Sorry there is a backlog of cases, the Doctor will see you when she can", "But Jen, I only wanted a cup of tea".

Those who know me well, will be aware I served on HMS Eskimo, nicknamed the "Mighty Mo", and I have been fortunate to call on my own "Mo" friends to help me on my journey. Led by Mo (Tivation), they have been instrumental in my fight to regain Mo (Shun), Mo (V'ment), and most importantly Mo (Billy T). Admittedly at times they needed the assistance of my good friend and ally, Mo (Feen). My very own Mo Band of Brothers.

First Physio session yesterday since I finished radiotherapy, I was hopeful the strength in my legs would be back to pre-radiotherapy levels which would allow me to abandon my cartoon characterisation of Bambi in the opening sequences of the film whenever I tried to walk. As it turned out, they are close to what they were!!!!!! Walked 100 metres and did a number of step-ups, all of which felt great and make me confident that I will be home this side of Christmas. :)

My Moobs are coming along nicely, thanks for asking - Though I am optimistic as the radiotherapy treatment kicks in and the pain in my spine reduces, I can start working my core muscles to limit the emergence of my pot-belly. I already feel like a 3 pints a night man, need to make sure it doesn't increase to the girth of a 20 pint a night drinker.

Normally weekends are a physio-free zone, but think I will partake of a couple of private sessions to further test my leg strength and reinforce my ambition to be home before Christmas.

From the Opulence of Offerton, enjoy yourselves wherever you are.

Tony, brother, on The Wilsons WhatsApp: Thinking positive Doctor Jen that your Dad will be home for Christmas xxx

Tug Gram 59

As we begin what I hope will be my last full week of incarceration as a guest of Her Majesty's Hospitals, I remain quietly optimistic that my strength is returning and I will have sufficient mobility to outrun the ward staff if they fire the starting pistol next week. :)

That said I was given a reminder last night of why it might not happen, with a long and arduous night of back pain. I thought I had been sensible by having a dose of morphine before I retired, but God has his little ways of reminding us who is in charge and last night his methodology to remind me he calls the shots was severe backache and Spasticity in my legs. It's my own fault really, my stroke will be 5 years old 30th January 2021, I remain convinced the stroke was cast upon me like an errant sinner because I had been spotted watching Man U on TV. This was Gods way of saying "You're a Scouser, do not meddle with destiny by watching the impure at play, have a stroke you ijiit"

Last night I chanced destiny again and watched the Manchester Derby, only to be blighted by a double whammy, a sh*t game and a night of pain.

Pass me the Morphine :)

Nevertheless I remain optimistic for a discharge next week. Whether the discharge celebrations will include a reunion with the family is unclear, as Olivia has been told to isolate due to her school bubble being breached by Covid. I just think bring it on, after the last few years, I can ride-out a few more challenges

My weight continues to fall by a couple of Lbs each week, making me more convinced than ever that the 'Prostate Diet' has commercial value, I just need to work out how to distribute it. And Boris thinks he has got distribution problems with a No Deal Brexit :)

Tug Gram 60

Freshly showered following my morning coffee.

It was well worth buying a box of deluxe biscuits for the staff to have on their breaks, some would say bribery, I think of it as an investment.

At the same time as the biscuits I also bought a tin of filter coffee, so every morning I am presented with a slice of toast and a cafetiere of real coffee. Lovely :)

Now if they can just stretch to a glass of red wine in the evening, I'd consider moving in full time :)

I have a combined Physio and Occupational Health session mid-morning as the staff assess my ability to mobilise and care for myself, prior to discharge. Mobility wise, I am very confident that my strength is back or close to pre-radiotherapy levels, but managing pain is another thing. I think everyone believes the pain is only short term, but the staff will be reluctant to let me go if I am still reliant on controlled drugs like liquid morphine. I shall remain optimistic .... or high :)

It is more likely that with my long hair (been a while since Angie has been able to work her magic with her shears) and my growing belly, they will ask me to stop shaving for a few days (hair does seem to grow fast under this drug regime), give me a red hospital gown, teach me to say Ho Ho Ho in a Manc accent so the inmates can understand me, and task me with handing out gifts on Christmas morning. As long as they leave a drink for Santa - I can cope with that duty watch :)

Smashed Physio, the staff have a combined (all disciplines) meeting later today when they review progress of individuals, so fingers crossed. They have also scheduled a home visit tomorrow to review my abode from a safety perspective to see what adaptations I need, if any, to move about my bungalow independently. :)

Tug Gram 61

76 days after I walked out of my house, well wheeled out on a stretcher by paramedics, I finally returned home. Okay only for an hour whilst the Occupational Health therapists reviewed my abode - was like being in an episode of "Who lives in a House like this" - to see if it was safe for me to return to.

And the computer said YES!!! :)

So my discharge date is set for the 21st December, contingent upon having enablement services in place. I assume enablement services are those people who go round at the end of an episode of WLIHLT* saying, let's look at the clues :)

It felt strange walking back up my drive, but not as emotionally charged as when I came back after my stroke, and that was only 8 weeks in hospital. Nevertheless it felt strange, and a bit like going round somebody else's house. At least as part of my review I got to lie on my new bed, which was delivered just after I was admitted to hospital 11 weeks ago, I'm pleased to say it felt comfortable. It felt strange to walk on carpets rather than hospital ward linoleum, and even stranger to have someone critique your own home. :)

The next few days will be a continued focus on strength building to ensure my legs not only look nice (as per my Glaswegian nurses detailed in Tug Gram 31), but that can support me for an extended period or over an extended distance. I shall be sensible and rest for the remainder of today, then hit the physio with gusto tomorrow.

Enjoy your day, Peeps.

Tug Gram 62

My first full day reflecting on the fact I have a discharge date and am close to going home, it feels strange. I am of course elated to be going home, but recognise I have become a little institutionalised by my time in hospital. If I get a headache after my discharge, I shall go to my medicine cabinet and quote my DOB, full name and 1st line of my address before I take out my aspirin. Likewise I will serve myself weak tea, and challenge myself every day why I don't take sugar, as I now know my body needs sugar to survive, and don't get me started at the need to strip my bed at 7.30am irrespective of whether I am still in it or not.

So it will be good to get home and enjoy for longer, the taste of what I had on my home visit yesterday. I've met some lovely people, but trust me with due apologies I shan't miss them :)

Physio again later, last few days of building strength in my legs, during which hopefully, the effects of the radiotherapy is also wearing off so my mobility will naturally improve as that happens and my spinal cord returns to normal.

My mate Mo Feen has been consigned to history for the last couple of days, another indication that my spinal column is responding to the radiotherapy. Hopefully, Mo and his band of brothers, will fade into the mists of time as my life attains some form of normality. Well as normal as an ex-matelot, stroke surviving, widower can be :)

I think I can say without fear of contradiction that it has been a life changing experience over the last few weeks, not one I am in a rush to repeat, but it has been interesting. :) With luck I have used up my supply of misfortune and going forward I shall be blessed with happy events and bucketloads of red wine :) Enjoy your day :)

Tug Gram 63

A tough physio session yesterday, lots of walking and steps, just what I need, same again today please :)

A third night without my mate Mo Feen, and slept very well, woke up a few times, but I believe that was due to the uncomfortable beds and routine hospital noises rather than any residual discomfort from my tumour. So really beginning to believe I am seeing the green shoots of recovery from radiotherapy, which augers well for improvements in my mobility.

Overall I would say, "It's beginning to look a lot like discharge" :)

Christmas shop will be delivered 21st, haircut booked for 22nd (I shall miss those silver curls) and family arriving soon after, Covid depending. What more could you ask for? :)

It will feel strange not being in a hospital environment, with its 24/7 buzz and movement. Going home will be like the first night on a ship after a long deployment and you are alongside engines and air conditioning shut down, you almost miss the hum of the engines, but after a few days you acclimatise and appreciate the silence. Anyway it won't be silent for long, not when that human tornado Olivia arrives, especially now she will be accompanied by her Elaine looky-likey partner in crime, Sara. Enjoy your day everyone :)

Tug Gram 64

Nearly the end of the Tug Gram odyssey as I stare down the barrel of my discharge after 11 weeks in the care of her Majesty's Hospitals. Great Physio session yesterday, walked round the outside of the building and through the garden to get me used to walking on different surfaces again, and to feel wind on my face. That aspect, the cold wind in my face, was the most exhilarating. 11 weeks since I had felt fresh air unless you count the short journeys on stretchers between hospitals as one had enough of me and passed me on to the next in the chain.

3rd Hormone injection yesterday, so one step closer to my menopause. Kept checking my Adam's Apple to make sure they hadn't lied to me and injected me with hormone replacement, but the Adams Apple was still there, and I hadn't started to sing in Falsetto, so maybe it is just hormone suppressant after all.

Last day of supervised hospital Physio today, will make sure I get my money's worth. Though will probably do a couple of private sessions over the weekend to make sure my mate prostate knows who is in charge. He might be developing Moobs and a Pot Belly, but I still own the rest of me. :)

It's been a rollercoaster of a journey, and not one I shall rush to do again, nevertheless it has been interesting, memorable and will definitely form part of my life's rich tapestry. Enjoy your day and have a great weekend. :)

Tug Gram 65

Day 80 in the Big Brother House, and fast approaching my eviction from the fun-filled Pantheon that is the Devonshire Unit here in Offerton, Stockport.

My remaining tenure can now be measured in hours not days, and I am in that period when I am doing things for the last time. Yesterday was the last supervised Physio, today will be the last weekly weigh-in. Each of these activities an integral part of my life for the best part of the past 11 weeks, but will cease with an abrupt end come Monday.

I have my friend Charley at the house when I return, and Dr Jenni will head over after Uni on Monday evening, Charley will help me settle in at home and Dr J. will manage my first evening outside the cosseted environment that is the NHS. I am glad I have someone at the house when I return, because I still believe the silence will be the singular most difficult aspect to adjust to when I return.

That said after a few days of tiny Typhoon Olivia and sister Sara, I may be begging for silence. :)

Need a shave this morning. Great, further proof that the injection was not hormone replacement, and was indeed hormone suppressant. I shan't need to take up knitting or craftwork as part of my long-term therapy. ... and hopefully I won't suddenly enjoy shopping.

With luck my last Saturday on the ward will be uneventful, and I can start to plan for a life after hospital, albeit a life with future oncology interventions intended to ensure my demise is most certainly due to very, very, old age. :)

Have a great weekend everyone out there in the wide world, hope your Christmas preparations are completed, and you are now beginning that slow wind down to the festive season. If not, shame on you, anyone would think you've been in hospital.

Tug Gram 66

Hopefully this is my last full day in hospital before heading home tomorrow, I won't say it's been a blast, but it's certainly had its moments and there are aspects I shall remember for a long time. :)

I think I shall do some recordings on my iPhone to take away with me, sounds that may comfort me during the silent hours when I can't sleep.

Sounds like a multiple and continuous 'nurses call'. The number of times I have been woken from a deep sleep by the "Action Stations" Klaxon on a ship, ready to drag myself out of my bed and run (As if I could run with my mates Stroke and Tumour) to my Action station in the Ships Communications Office, only to realise it was someone calling for a pee bottle using the nurses call button. :)

Or sounds like the approaching noise of the Blood Pressure machine, as well as the BP machine itself. The BP trolley coming down the corridor to the ward sounded like the approach of a Chieftain tank, and once the cuff was on an arm, it sounded the Morse code for the letters S and I. I could hear .../.. in my head for hours after they had taken observations.

Don't get me started on Medicine Rounds, the nurses without fail were trained to abuse me when they distributed medicines, in my case daily injections and drugs. They all without exception would start the routine with abuse, I was like with an inmate at Guantanamo Bay under interrogation, they would look at me and mouth, "Just a little prick." Hurtful on so many levels. :)

Christmas for us, like for thousands in the UK, has fundamentally changed. Rob is in tier 4, so cannot travel, and Jenni has to follow the new restrictions. Nevertheless we shall make the best of the festive period, make maximum use of FaceTime, and plan for a celebratory weekend somewhere when all of this is under control and we have returned to a degree of normality. :)

Still life is not all bad. Liverpool won 7-0 yesterday, which is so ironic because I entered hospital on the back of a 7-2 defeat for Liverpool FC so many moons ago. Who says Karma is a figment of imagination. Enjoy your Sunday folks. :)

Tug Gram 67

Back Home was an iconic football song sung by the 1970 England World Cup team, led by Bobby Moore, and will be remembered by those of a certain age. Back Home was also my mantra yesterday as I sat on my own couch, watched my own TV and slept in my own bed for literally the first time. Wonderful to be home, if a tad daunting as I tried to recall how to manage complicated activities such as turning on the television and resetting the heating.

I have been assessed by the local Home Care team to identify my needs and they will put forward care suggestions, but it was positive that they believe I am making solid progress towards self-sufficiency. In the meantime I am being looked after by my daughter Doctor Jenni, love her to bits and she is doing a sterling job, but obviously did not bring her kid gloves.

My cleaner has been and worked her magic, additionally she has cut off my silver curls, and I cannot tell you how good that feels. :)

Thank you to everyone for their goodwill messages and also for the many Christmas Cards I have received. I will certainly respond to the online messages, but confess my ability to send Christmas cards this year is severely restricted. Please accept my apologies, and assurances that normal service will be resumed in 2021.

Tug Grams will now be parked until at least after Christmas as I continue to rebuild my mobility and strive to restore my walking and movement back to pre-tumour levels.

Have a fantastic, peaceful and plentiful Christmas in whatever location or Tier you find yourselves in, hopefully 2021 will be a much better year for us all. :)

Home. At long last.

Jacqui, sister, on The Wilsons WhatsApp: xx

Claire, sister, on The Wilsons WhatsApp: Brilliant xxx

Emma, niece, on The Wilsons WhatsApp: :/

Rita, sister, on The Wilsons WhatsApp: I think you have missed your mouth Phil, some xmas pud on your head xxx

Tony, brother, on The Wilsons WhatsApp: Looking good Phil. Good to see you back home

Becky, niece, on The Wilsons WhatsApp: Love this! xxx

Tug Gram 68

So Christmas is behind us, an enjoyable family period when I was looked after superbly by Dr Jenni and boyfriend Chris, thank you both, as well as being licked to death by that Wolfhound in disguise, Eric the Wire Haired Vizsla.

All augmented with frequent FT calls from the granddaughters. Olivia was her usual funny chatty self, and Sara just painted her face with whatever meal she was eating. Priceless :)

Have the Care teams coming in today, and just done my first home physio routine since leaving hospital. :)

Now for a well-earned coffee :)

Mo Feen has not been sighted since well before Christmas, and Bambi's Ice is a bit firmer so whilst I still tire easily, I believe my walking is getting better. Have a great day :)

Tug Gram 69

Spent the last couple of days testing my ability to manage by myself, and I am pleased to say things are going in the right direction. I don't see myself joining Dr Jenni on her 100-mile run anytime soon, but as each day passes and the effects of

the radiotherapy recedes, I may be up for a 100 metre hobble
:)

I have managed to shower unaided without drowning or falling, albeit with advice from Dr Jenni to establish a routine with chairs and towels that enable me to move from the shower safely and to dry myself.

Dr Jenni has also reintroduced the awarding of achievement badges for developing new skills, over Christmas I was awarded my tea/coffee making badge, as well as my breakfast preparation and shower badge. Yesterday my gorgeous Glaswegian friend and old Northwood shipmate Lucanne witnessed me achieve the 'Technology' badge when I managed to switch between 2 applications on my iPhone, without cutting our call - You wouldn't believe I spent 20 years working in the mobile phone industry.

Yesterday also saw the reintroduction of unsupervised physio using bed exercises set by the physiotherapist when in the Devonshire Unit, took me 30 minutes and left me exhausted, but extremely satisfied. Same again today. My final self-imposed challenge (other than the one about finishing that box of chocolates) was to cook myself a meal. I took it easy by starting with a pizza for lunch, but yesterday evening it was a rice concoction (guaranteed to be healthy as it was provided by Dr Jenni) and steamed vegetables. Lovely - To top it all, I got my washing-up badge afterwards. :)

Just moving around the kitchen brought home my immediate dilemma. I need my good right arm to hold my stick to stay upright, which leaves my weak left arm (which is even weaker after 12 weeks of no exercise) to move plates etc around the kitchen. My current solution is to simply eat wherever I cook my food, but greater movement and control is definitely high on my agenda.

Please note this is NOT a plea for mobility solutions to make my life easier. I don't mind if you bring mobility aids to my attention, but you must accept that I come from the school of "Just keep trying to do things naturally, until you can do things properly" :)

I am really optimistic that I will continue to improve, nevertheless I am very grateful for the offers of assistance from my friends and family. Additionally I appreciate the opportunity to share my progress and frustrations with old Navy shipmates - like Pat Jones, Julie Walsh, and more recently Lucanne.

I trust your New Year's Eve will not be blighted by Covid-19 restrictions, but in any instance, may your evening be full of fun as we look forward to a much better 2021 (at least once the vaccine is rolled out :)

Tug Gram 70

2021, who'd have thought it would ever get here, and who amongst us is missing 2020?

I spent a very civilized New Year's Eve like most of the UK, at home celebrating the New Year with a large glass of Red …Will not even try to pretend I was still awake at midnight to see the New Year in, like most days, my wick was well and truly burnt out by 8pm. At least I was able to set my 2021 resolution, but no prizes for guessing it was around improved mobility and ability to walk unaided, both of which are expected to arrive early in 2021 if I have anything to do with it. :)

Even though it is officially a public holiday today, no rest for the wicked, so bed Physio will be completed this morning. To be clear for those whose mindset never gets above their navel, this is not a euphemism for sex, rather it is for exercises designed to strengthen my legs whilst laying on the bed so I don't put further pressure on my spine. :)

Had a great day yesterday, completed my bed Physio, but also tested myself walking round the kitchen completely unaided. Managed 10 widths of the kitchen without my stick, which augers well for getting my food from the microwave to the table, AND more importantly I get my "Kitchen Walking badge" Also had a Med's review call with the Doctors surgery, when they wanted me to monitor my own blood pressure, sadly all I achieved was to tie my right arm and the blood pressure monitor in knots, so no one-armed BP reading badge. :)

I also enquired if my pot-belly would disappear once my body adjusted to the cancer drugs, but Dr Jenni suggested my pot-belly was more likely a result of the industrial amounts of Christmas pudding and chocolate log I had consumed since coming home. Mmmmmm she may have a point, but Swiss roll covered in half-inch thick chocolate, what isn't there to like? I rest my case M'lud, Moobs and Pot-belly it is then.

Who knows what is in store for us in 2021, but I certainly hope it is an improvement on 2020. Not sure what was worse Covid or cancer, but at least Liverpool won the league. Have a great 2021 everyone :)

Tug Gram 71

For two millennia man has followed the principle set by big G of working for 6 days and resting on the 7th, then along came the EU Working Time directive that brought us the 5 day working week. I have decided to stick with the EU philosophy and exercise for 5 days and rest for 2, so no physio today. YAY...

Did my physio yesterday and also tested myself by repeatedly walking around or across my kitchen unaided, so whilst my muscles are a touch stiff this morning, no real pain or discomfort. Mo Feen is just a distant memory, and long may he remain so. I have a supply of morphine at home to use if I need it, but hopefully the bottle will just gather dust as I improve my mobility without excessive pain!!! May look to sell the bottle to the local drug dealer rather than let it go to waste. :)

As I said I spent some time yesterday walking unaided round my kitchen, though maybe I was a tad ambitious when I decided to carry a cup of tea from my kitchen to the lounge, though the exercise did earn me my mopping up the spilt tea badge.

Going to have a couple of days rest then return to the physio regime on Monday, I am now extremely positive that I will get back to my pre-tumour self. I am far more stable, and no longer do I dance from one side of the room to the other as I try to recover my balance. Also my gait has developed into stumbling Neanderthal and less newborn Bambi, so progress there. Things can only get better. Have a great weekend everybody. :)

Tug Gram 72

'72 the year I joined up :)

Rangers won yesterday (come on Stevie G, who said a red couldn't love a blue). Man United won again with a dubious penalty (and I said Pogba couldn't even trip over his own feet, how wrong I was), now all we need is for Liverpool to beat the Saints tomorrow, and world order is restored.

Received a lovely Christmas box yesterday, it was supposed to have been hand delivered by Rob & Ellen, but Covid tier 4 put paid to that. Nevertheless it was lovely to receive, amongst other gifts, my body weight in chocolate bars (They know me so well!), and some delightful and personal fridge magnets. Magnets that included a shot of the first time I held Granddaughter Sara, a similar one for Elaine, and some early year photos of Sara and Olivia, as well as a group family shot on one of our Forest holidays. :)

I felt quite emotional as I shuffled the magnets and saw the pictures of those who mean so much to me, and though I doubted that my resolve could be hardened further, it made me more determined than ever to overcome this latest setback and regain my mobility.

I reflected that my tumour has most definitely "done one" now, and whilst the benefits from the radiotherapy will be gradual, they are assuredly on the way. So that leaves the minor matter of my dealing with the prostate cancer, and making sure it doesn't control my life.

That process starts with improvements to my walking, ditching my quad walking stick for a normal walking stick, and increasing my walking unaided round the house. Neanderthal man has only recently arrived, but he has to go. In my mind I can hear my Navy Drill instructor shouting for me to stand tall and push my chest out, so that will be mantra going forward. Sadly he also said I would never be able to march in a million years, but I made the guard platoon, so I shall ignore that bit :)

The magnets were a reminder I have so much to live for, and improvements to my mobility will enable me to enjoy whose who are close to me. I have always insisted that I will not be a victim of circumstances, and will never be an invalid, now is the time for me to do my part and get my body more compliant :) Have a great Sunday Y'all.

Jacqui, sister, on The Wilsons WhatsApp: Go Phil! Your positivity, resilience and mental attitude is inspiring xxx

Becky, niece, on The Wilsons WhatsApp: Couldn't agree more! Amazing! xxx

Tug Gram 73

Been up and at 'em early today :) Stripped my bed, and got the bedding in the wash, arranged my MOT and just about to complete my physio routine :)

As I threatened yesterday, now walking with the aid of a normal walking stick rather than the more stable quad stick. So far so good :)It requires a greater degree of concentration, but is the next logical step in my recovery.

Will use this stick for a couple of weeks until I am more stable then will increase the distances indoors, I walk without a stick, see what that brings me and just hope it is not a flattened nose.

Feeling incredibly positive about my recovery, less so unfortunately about Liverpool -v- Southampton game tonight :) Have a great day everyone :)

Tug Gram 74

It has been 2 days since I retired the quad-walking stick, and started using a standard walking stick. Pleased to say I haven't fallen yet, so my nose retains its normal shape :) It is more difficult, I have to concentrate all of the time, but if it was meant to be easy God would have fitted wheels to my feet and made me a Segway.

One consequence of using the standard stick is I have reawakened muscles that have lain dormant since I went into Salford Royal. This means I have to work harder when I walk, but also means the reintroduction of muscle spasms at night. Once again, I am like a one-legged auditionee for Riverdance as I twitch and flex on the mattress. At least now, thanks to my physios and Aneta, I know how to counter the condition. Hopefully the spasms will ease once my muscles regain strength.

Sadly my muscle spasms had more life in them than Liverpool when they played Southampton on Monday, and we deservedly lost the game. I should see the game as a sign that things are returning to normal.

Stretched my cuisine skills last night and made myself a cheese omelette, very tasty though I say it myself, and there was something very satisfying about having to wash the dishes afterwards rather than just place containers in the recycling bins. :)

Will complete Physio shortly, then give myself a well-earned coffee before entering day 2 of lockdown, which means absolutely no going out for me. As if I did. Have a great day everybody. :)

Tug Gram 75

Wishing my older brother Tony a very happy birthday today, we shall make it for a beer as soon as this lockdown is over. :)

Another day yesterday using a standard walking stick, it remained tough and without doubt stretches me, but I believe the fact it is so difficult means ultimately it will do me some good. If nothing else it follows the mantra no pain, no gain. Also completed my daily physio, and will do so again today, again in this cold weather, it is difficult, but I will persevere and hope that once I enter the outreach Physio programme I will be stretched (not literally!) and worked hard to improve my mobility and get me back to where I was before the tumour ate my spinal cord.

My Granddaughter's Olivia and Sara celebrated Kings Day yesterday, which for them means a 2nd Christmas Day. The benefit of an English father and Spanish mother, I just hope that next year the English and Spanish grandfathers are able to travel and be part of the celebrations. In any instance it was heart-warming to see the photographs and videos of them both opening and playing with Kings Day presents.

I am still incredibly positive about my recovery, I remain in contact with a couple of the nurses who either looked after me when I had my Stroke, or more recently my cancer diagnosis. It would be a lie to say there weren't dark moments as I took in the stroke, then some years later the spinal tumour and almost immediately after that the prostate cancer condition. Nevertheless when I receive messages and good wishes from young nurses like Erin, who despite her workload in this pandemic, takes time to reach out to me and wish me well, it makes me feel good and inspires me to work harder. So I refuse to accept the limitations of my conditions, but trust me that is not the same as Donald Trump refusing to accept the US presidential election result. No protesting outside my house whilst I do my physio. :)

The restrictions of the lockdown mean no new badges earned this week, nevertheless I shall continue to seek opportunities to gain new badges and make further improvements. :)

Tug Gram 76

Happy Birthday to my gorgeous daughter Jenni, both of our children have been incredibly supportive of me during my recent troubles, but it is fair to say Jenni being that bit closer (2 hours away) has borne the brunt. Especially in the early days of my hospitalization when she would regularly replenish my laundry. Just a simple 4 or 5 hour round trip. :) As their Father, I couldn't be more prouder of them both. :)

Have a fantastic day today Jen with Chris and Eric (for those whose imaginations are going into overdrive at the mention of Chris and Eric, it is not some kind of Ménage a trois, Eric is their dog!).

It is nearly 2 years since I lost Elaine, but I know she would be looking down today and reflecting how blessed we are to have 2 such wonderful children. I also know if I went to a seance, the clairvoyant would be asking "Does anyone know an Elaine, she wants you to understand they get their brains and looks from the mother, you know!"

Weekend, so in time honoured fashion, no physio today, but as it is the weekend, I also allow myself 3 cups of coffee instead of my daily 2, which means I will get my daily exercise from repeated trips to the toilet.

I have to reduce my liquid intake in the evening, otherwise my bathroom light is going on and off so frequently during the night, every Boy Scout on the estate has got their Morse Code badge.

Talking of which, I am claiming my tin-opening badge :) Yesterday I opened a tin of peas completely unaided, and without a safety net. :)

I also received a text from a friend yesterday who has only just heard of my latest troubles, she asked me how I was feeling. Having recently come out of the shower (unaided, another badge).

Have a great weekend everyone, and Jen enjoy your birthday. I shall roast a hog in your honour (well have a special Wiltshire Farm Foods meal), and may even open a bottle of Red to celebrate for you :)

Tug Gram 77

Another number that has great significance for me as it was in 1977 that I married Elaine, and was fortunate to spend the next 41 years as her husband before she passed nearly 21 months ago.

In Tug Gram 76 I committed the most heinous of sins, a grammatical assault of epic proportions when I wrote "I couldn't be more prouder of them both". I await the subpoena from the Court of Grammatical Corrections led by my English teacher Niece Becky, a Commissioner in waiting for the Grammar Police, the scourge of incorrectly used apostrophes and other grammatical crimes.

On a more positive note I set a new world record yesterday walking 25 steps without my walking stick (the Quad stick has been confined to the annals of history), and for the last 11 of those steps I was carrying a full cup of coffee. Okay it was with my good arm so maybe not quite a circus act in its own right, even though again, I didn't use a safety net. :)

I have decided Mr Prostrate like Mr Stroke before him has a twisted sense of humour.

I submit M'Lud as evidence of his grossly unfair practices the following:

Before a shower I can drink 3 cups of coffee and be at the furthest point from the facilities, safe in the knowledge that any accidental spillages won't matter, I will be changing my clothes after the shower anyway. Outcome is never a drop spilled, I am drier than a camel crossing the Kalahari Desert, and I always make the facilities irrespective of how slow I am.

After a shower, and dressed in fresh clothes and underwear having had nothing to drink for at least an hour, and be stood next to the toilet. Feel the need to go and the outcome is a flood of biblical proportions that would overcome an entire packet of Tena Pads, resulting in another trip to the underwear drawer.

I rest my case; my prostate cancer behaves in a way that defies good manners and proves he has an ornery disposition just like my stroke before him.

Some of you may recall I wrote a 2nd book during the first, or was it the 400th, lockdown. :) Anyhow I submitted the manuscript to my aforementioned Niece, Becky, whose comments on my first draft were along the lines of "Do not pass Go, Do not collect £200, Uncle is a Loser!" Additionally the manuscript was covered in more red ink than a kid's depiction of a Middle Eastern Sea. Thankfully, my final draft received a 9.9 out of 10, which trust me, automatically places me on the Righthand side of God. So I shall publish "Learning to Love your Stroke", and be damned. No prizes though for guessing the subject matter!! Watch this space for publication details :)

Tug Gram 78

Thank you to those of you who pointed out my grammatical errors in yesterday's Tug Gram in the form of Prostrate rather than Prostate. I am thinking of starting a daily competition based on the Tug Gram's, first to find 5 grammatical errors wins a prize. Currently the Star prize for finding 5 errors is to be immediately Unfriended on Facebook, and purged from my life forever. Great, I hear you say. :)

It is becoming less of a Tug Gram, more of a "What's the Wally done today?" :)

I blame slight Aphasia remaining from my Stroke, or was it the aftereffects of too much Morphine after the cancer, not sure. I'll have to check what excuse I am up to in my "Feeble reasons for Failure manual 2020."

My neighbour and friend Sabrina has got into the achievement badges. She achieved her "Taking Blood Pressure" badge yesterday, as she monitored my blood Pressure levels following a request from my GP's surgery. You may recall I did try to do it with my one working arm, but all I achieved was getting my reef knot badge as I wrapped the monitor into exotic (but totally unworkable) shapes on my arm. :) Anyway Sabrina to the rescue, not sure she needed to wear her Ann Summers Nurses uniform, but at least it meant I got a high reading.

Had my Wiltshire Farm Foods Sunday Roast after my daily FT call with the family, led of course by Olivia & Sara. Without sounding like a field representative for WFF, the quality of the food is excellent and it means I can drag my meal from the microwave onto the kitchen work surface until I am ready to apply for my Waiter Badge, and carry my meals to the table. :)

Making good progress on self-publishing "Learning to Love your Stroke" on Amazon, or to be more accurate, Rob is. Thanks Rob. :)

My cleaners visit today, the "Scrubbers are on the Plot" is a frequent refrain when they visit from Jackie my x-neighbour, luckily Angie and Joan have a fantastic sense of humour and take the banter in good stead. Anyway I hope they will be able to tackle the ironing mountain, which is reminiscent of the EU Butter Mountains from the 70's until such time as I am able to try for my ironing badge. In addition, they will major in their normal activities of drinking coffee and chatting like those characters in a Les Dawson comedy sketch, Cissie & Ada.

Have a great week everyone :)

Tug Gram 79

Must have been the worst night in a long time last night, still awake at 2am. I sleep on a King sized bed with a memory foam mattress, and I must have covered every inch of the mattress as I tried to get comfortable. The memory foam mattress must have thought they were coping with the Brigade of Guards, I was moving around so much. :)

It was a night when both my legs and left arm were painful, whether in response to the exercise I had completed during the previous day or a result of my reducing my pain relief to just 1 paracetamol tablet morning and evening. In any instance I did look longingly at the drawer which contains my home stash of morphine, but I resisted and am glad I did.

Once the pain eased the limbs started uncontrollable twitching like an uncoordinated attempt at RiverDance. The last time so many twitches were seen in the UK was when a Lesser Spotted Woodpecker was spotted on our shores.

(And you thought the only rare bird I knew of was the lone female touting her wares amongst the She-male Kaities in Bugis Street Singapore in the 70's) :) I shall complete my daily physio routine this morning if only to prove to my incalcitrant limbs that I am in charge, and hope for a better night tonight. I must have been delirious during the night, because I swear I heard the mattress shouting "One at a time please" as I rolled around in pain. On another occasion the mattress asked if the leader of the Khmer Rouge, you know Pol Pot Belly, was on the mattress.

So complete my physio, enjoy a coffee then complete the process of ordering my new book "Learning to Love your Stroke"

Have a great day everyone, remember pain is just Gods way of telling you, you are still alive. :)

Jacqui, sister, on The Wilsons WhatsApp: Look forward to reading your next book and I think you should make tug grams into a book too xxx

Becky, niece, on The Wilsons WhatsApp: I've been saving all Phil's entries into a diary for him xxx

Nicola, niece, on The Wilsons WhatsApp: International bestseller coming soon.

Tug Gram 80

My 2nd pain free night in a row, Yippee, so slept better, although Monsieur Prostate ensured I only slept for 3 or 4 hours at a time. Nevertheless that was good for me, unfortunately less so for the Boy Scouts on the estate. Having achieved their Morse code badges from the flashes of my toilet light going on and off, the increase in light usage caused by my efforts to both rehydrate and satisfy Monsieur Prostate has generated what appears to be a random code that leaves the Boy Scouts wandering around the estate with a bemused expression thinking they have a Russian spy in the midst. :)

Yesterday also produced a new world record as I walked totally unaided from one side of the house to the other. 75 steps in total, not sure the speed of my movement will have Usain Bolt worrying about his world records, but it felt good for me, though not as good as the Fosbury Flop I did on the couch at the end (just the flop, not the leap)

District nurse coming today to administer my latest cancer jab to suppress my hormones. I always envisage the drug entering my system and at the same time my Moobs enlarging at the same rate. Anyway that's my excuse and I'm sticking to it :) it's just a pity that the blood extracted doesn't reduce my potbelly by an equal amount.

MacMillan nurses visiting today as well, maybe I'll get some idea of life expectancy. I just hope that it extends beyond the Liverpool-v- Man U game on Sunday, but then again the way Ole has Man U playing, maybe not. Have a great day everyone, remember worse things happen at sea (so they say)

Tug Gram 81

Another decent sleep, Monsieur Prostate had a few niggles early on and my left leg was twitching like a radio operator on a Morse key, but once I settled, it was into a deep sleep. :)

I am surprised that I am sleeping so well given the significance of this weekend, I am sure some of you will be living in blissful ignorance of the monumental event scheduled to take place this coming Sunday as Man United take on 2nd place, and current league champions (just in case you hadn't heard) Liverpool FC!

I shall spend the weekend like an 18th Century Missionary travelling amongst the pagans of Manchester who cover themselves in red in homage to the one true god, Bill Shankly. I shall preach to the heathens who worship the false gods of Old Trafford. I shall try to convert them to the righteous path as trod by deities such as Sir Kenny, and Herr Juergen. I shall try to teach them the error of their ways in attending mass services at the Theatre of Dreams rather than the more celestial Anfield.

Oh well, I can continue to dream can't I? In truth I am already hoping for a draw on Sunday just to avoid defeat :)

I am close to being discharged by the Social Services outreach team, whose brief is to ensure an individual has a good level of self-sufficiency and able to manage themselves in a safe manner. Their view is that my determination to be self-sufficient is paying dividends, and with my agreement they believe other patients need them more. They agree with me that what I need is more directed physio to rebuild strength in my legs to improve my walking. So another step on the road to recovery :)

Woke this morning to a message from one of the nurses who looked after me during my tumour operation and recovery. It was lovely to hear from Erin, but she and her colleagues are having a torrid time and struggling to cope in the pandemic. I hope as a nation we properly reward our NHS when this is over and recognise the efforts that so few are doing for so many. I for one say God bless the NHS :)

Weekend, but given I ducked a few days to see if I could ease the muscle pain, I shall do my physio this morning then enjoy my mandatory 3 weekend cups of coffee (followed by frequent trips to the bathroom, No pain, no gain…)

Have a great weekend everyone…

And so we arrive at my final Tug Gram for inclusion in this book – though it might please some to know that, due to the demand from my friends, family and fans, my Tug Grams have continued long after deciding on which would be the final one to feature in the book (just yesterday, I shared Tug Gram 150!).

The final one, 82, in the book comes from Sunday 17th January 2021 – almost 4 months since the day my legs gave way underneath me. So why stop at Tug Gram #82 some of you may ask, while others may insist, I should have stopped at #1; the answer is simple: my journey, as such, is complete. Henceforth, we are into the mundane with regular, repetitive exercise and medication - all designed to slowly bring about my recovery. I will continue both my medical regimen and my exercise programme, but I believe I can only improve going forward. I will continue to track my progress, and will remain grateful to everyone who touched my cancer journey. I look forward to the day my life does not revolve around my cancer diagnosis, but in the meantime I will continue to live my life secure in the knowledge there isn't much more that can be thrown my way!

Tug Gram 82

Wow, slept like a log and even Monsieur Prostate didn't interrupt my slumbers. It must be the excitement now the great day has arrived.

No, not Christmas, that was last month.

No, Easter is a few months away when we celebrate the end of Covid.

I know the kids and grandchildren's birthdays are special, but so is this.

Yes, even more important than the Queens Official Birthday, it's Liverpool versus Manchester United :)

Some of you are asking why my cancer is French (Monsieur Prostate), and the answer is simple. My cancer is stubbornly refusing to move, knows just when and how to hurt me (Don't think you're forgiven for the Hundred Years' War, Frenchie), and will open migrant centres in other parts of my body without permission. Yes, I know they are tumours and not the fault of France, but it is funny to read this in a French accent like in Allo, Allo. Okay!!

Anyway much to celebrate in downtown Woodley here in Stockport. I got my Mobile Technicians badge yesterday, when after taking receipt of a new iPhone 11, I was able to successfully migrate my personal data without a safety net - I also won the family lockdown quiz YAY!! Mastermind, here I come, Rev up the black chair, John Humphrys

Prepared my questions yesterday for my Oncology appointment next week, the kids didn't think my first question "Can I send it back, if I don't like the cancer during the trial period" was appropriate so back to the keyboard...

And of course I published my 2nd book (Thanks for your help, Rob) - the feedback has been fantastic, thank you.

Have a fantastic Sunday everyone, I shall enjoy not doing physio for one day, and may enjoy the match later. Wherever you are, have fun :)

5. Living with Cancer

People ask me how I cope living with cancer, especially knowing it is at Stage 4 and metastatic, and there isn't a stage 5. The answer is incredibly easy, I ignore it. I know at some point it will come back to bite me, but until we reach that point, Monsieur Prostate and I will live in perfect disharmony. I accept that my cancer is incurable, but focus on the fact it is treatable, albeit the medication is effective for circa two years, nevertheless I trust that by the time one medication becomes ineffective, another treatment is ready to manage my condition.

In the meantime, I shall stay as fit as possible, improve my mobility, and enjoy time with my children and lovely grandchildren, Olivia and Sara.

One of my oncology team told me the record for surviving with stage 4 metastatic prostate cancer was 25 years. I decided I would aim for 50 years, which would make me 115 years old, and maybe struggling with the physio, but what the hell!

Despite the potential longevity of me and my condition, the MacMillan nurses wanted to know my wishes for when things deteriorate, specifically where do I want to spend my end of life care? Apparently, Pulau Tioman, a tropical Island I visited in 1974 is not an option. Pity, it was very nice.

6. Dedications

As I reflect on the past 12 months since my cancer diagnosis, I know I have so many people to be grateful for. Not least of which are my family, including my late, much missed Elaine, who remains a source of inspiration in my recovery as I imagine what she would say on those days I am struggling. Suffice to say it would not offer much by way of sympathy, but would encourage and cajole in equal measures. Then there is our children and their respective partners, Rob, Jenni, Ellen and Chris. I shall always remain in awe of their ability to be so wise and constructive at such tender ages. They have been through a lot in their short lives, and all I can say is I am immensely proud of how they deal with issues and remain positive.

I should also highlight some of the nursing staff who have helped me on my journey, starting with my local GP practice who remotely identified that something was amiss and encouraged me to call 999. I am grateful to Dr Lucy Higgins and Dr Gor for their diligence at a time during the pandemic when it would have been easier to defer any decision. Their intervention undoubtedly played a major role in ensuring I didn't worsen my spinal condition which could have led to permanent paralysis.

The paramedics who made an initial diagnosis, incorrect as it turned out, but nevertheless prompted them to bluelight me to a Specialist Medical Unit. Unfortunately, I was somewhat distracted so never knew their names, but rest assured I know I am in their debt.

Once I was under the care of Salford Royal Foundation Trust, I was treated with compassion and care at every juncture, well okay maybe not when the Ward Sister transferred me to the Covid ward. Because of my previous stroke, I knew I would struggle to retain and pass on key information to my family, but Erin O'Connell a trainee nurse took it upon herself to let my daughter know when I went down and returned from surgery. Doctors, specialist nurses and ward staff have all willingly and repeatedly spoken to my family to let them know of my progress, and this despite the constant pressures of their day jobs.

Having spent 8 weeks as an inpatient in another facility following my stroke in 2016, I fully expected to experience the same hit or miss treatment at Salford. A good leader on the ward meant quality treatment and care, a poor leader just meant the day or night would be long, painful, and leave you looking forward to shift changeover. At Salford Royal, however, I found the consistency in levels of care and attention by the leadership team amazing which left you totally confident in the system.

As an example Ward Sisters Vicky Carruthers and Natasha Vraka ran the ward with a regularity that is both reassuring and calming, but both would undertake the most menial of tasks if the need arose. They and Staff Nurses Yasmin Mellish, Kat Hunt, Rachel Roach, Hannah Lawless and Alice Duncombe appear unflappable. No matter how chaotic events on the ward, no matter how many buzzers from patients demanding immediate attention, they went about the business in a calm, efficient and reassuring manner. I couldn't respect these named individuals more for the work they do, and for consistently delivering to the gold standard of nursing. On one particularly difficult night on the ward, with a couple of really demanding patients, I asked Yasmin Mellish how she did it, what made her come back day after day. She responded that she treated every patient how she would want her family treated, and I genuinely believe this is a common mantra for all of the nursing teams. The best accolade I can offer the people I name in this chapter, is that they are not only fantastic NHS staff, but also wonderful empathetic human beings.

I can only assume somewhere in the depths of Salford Royal is a cloning machine that ensures they turn out homogeneous leaders, and also ensures their trainee nurses and ward support staff are gifted with the same comparable levels of capability. I was constantly amazed at the compassion and tenderness that young nurses like Erin and Izzy demonstrated to patients, some of whom at times were downright obnoxious, but the professionalism shown by these young ladies was exemplary. It is wonderful to see young people in a role they are ideally suited for.

I understand that after a traumatic event like the one I had undergone, it would be easy to overdramatize the levels of care received. Trust me when I say I am a level headed, pragmatic individual who wouldn't hesitate to complain if circumstances warranted it, but I feel privileged to have been looked after by this team of people.

That said I have met some amazing and caring human beings amongst our nursing and HCA communities. With only a couple of exceptions, both of whom appear to see the morning breakfast/wash and dress exercise as a race, as if they are paid for the speed they complete work, rather than patient well-being, the team are friendly compassionate and have a genuine interest in helping and caring for the patients.

I was then transferred to the Devonshire Unit in Stockport for intensive physiotherapy. Here again, I could not begin to express my appreciation at the care I have received from the likes of Heather, Neeta, Carol (nights), Alex, Svetlana (nights), and the other nursing staff. As a team they deliver exceptional care and will always have my thanks.

This excellence continued amongst the HCA community from people like Julie Wilkinson, Maria, Jenny and Ash all of whom take it upon themselves to go that extra mile and do whatever they can to improve the life of a patient. Maria, for example, took it upon herself to do my washing a couple of times and returned it washed, dried and folded. Julie always popped her head in to say hello and pass a few minutes with me. Jenny is just a delight to have around. You cannot believe how these little acts of kindness make such a difference.

Even amongst the catering and domestic teams, this level of care and compassion shines through. People like Becky who heard I didn't like instant coffee, so took it upon herself to make me a cafetière of coffee when she was on duty, or Sandra who knew I liked fresh fruit so brought me any spare fruit. Such acts of kindness make all the difference, and stand out for me as being the stellar acts of care from my nearly 12 weeks in hospital, five of which were at the Devonshire.

I was also incredibly impressed by the younger members of staff, Lauren, Erin and Jenny, whose level of empathy was all the more surprising and inspiring given their young years; the fact they are so compassionate tells me a lot about the training and mentorship offered by the Management team, as it does about the individuals.

Upon my discharge and return home my children were immense, but I was also fortunate to get support from my fellow veterans Lucanne Mackay who I served with at HMS Warrior, home of CINCFleet, and from HMS Mercury, Julie Walsh and Pat Jones. All three x-Wrens kept my spirits alive with regular online messages of support. I hope they recognise how much their communication meant to me in my darker times.

My physiotherapy continues to this day, and I am indebted to one of the most professional, compassionate and in truth, funny Physiotherapists I have had the pleasure to be treated by. Megan Knowles-Eade who is based at Neurological Physiotherapy in Cheadle Manchester has been instrumental in helping me refine my walking to the extent I no longer use a walking stick in my house, and my overall posture is massively improved. She has been a marvel for me, and as my treatment with her continues, I have every confidence that under her expert guidance, I will continue to prosper.

Words cannot express my gratitude to my children Rob and Jenni and everyone I have named in this chapter. In your own way, you helped me through the dark periods and helped me on my recovery journey. **Thank you**.

7. What's next?

As I reach the first anniversary of my cancer diagnosis, I consider myself fortunate to have encountered so many wonderful people and organisations as I look to recover my mobility and retain my independence.

Thank you for reading this book, and sharing my experiences. I hope my words help people realise serious conditions are not to be feared, but to be approached with fortitude and spirit and to embrace the excellent care you will be offered.

One final anecdote I must share with you was the conversation I had with one of the Personal Trainers from my local gym, he had read my second book *Learning to Love Your Stroke* in which I write about the benefits of gym visits on physical and mental well-being. He told me about a Charity media campaign led by Age UK, in which they would utilise real disabled people who used sport as a means of improving their life. I successfully applied to the company managing the project without really understanding what I was letting myself in for. Suffice to say, I was given the opportunity to share my story with a much wider audience, and whilst I am sure established actors have nothing to fear from my screen debut, it does appear to have resonated with everyone who has watched it. Because of my veteran background, I can truly say I have reached an international audience (albeit a small one) as my fellow veterans from around the globe have viewed the video on YouTube;

Find out more about my story, and the stories of others in similar situations by either visiting;

Youtube: https://youtu.be/Dj87wzfVxm8

https://weareundefeatable.co.uk/our-stories/phil

As I said previously, I know my cancer is incurable, but it is treatable, so although the treatments have a finite lifespan, I shall continue to focus on enjoying my life and spending as much time with family and friends as I can, especially my gorgeous granddaughters Olivia (6) and Sara (2)

Thank you for reading and I'd love to have your feedback so please don't hesitate to get in touch
undefeatable2021@gmail.com

Phil Wilson

October 2021

Printed in Great Britain
by Amazon